Cherry Cake
and
Ginger Beer

CHERRY CAKE
AND
GINGER BEER

JANE BROCKET

HODDER &
STOUGHTON

First published in Great Britain in 2008 by Hodder & Stoughton
An Hachette Livre UK company

6

Copyright © Jane Brocket 2008

The right of Jane Brocket to be identified as the Author of the Work has been
asserted by her in accordance with the Copyright, Designs and Patents Act 1988.

A CIP catalogue record for this title is available from the British Library

ISBN 978 0 340 96089 9

Typeset in MT Poliphilus

Printed and bound by Clays Ltd, St Ives plc

All Enid Blyton quotes in this publication are reproduced with kind permission of
Chorion Rights Limited, excluding pages 47–48 and 223–224. All rights reserved.

Hodder & Stoughton policy is to use papers that are natural, renewable and
recyclable products and made from wood grown in sustainable forests. The
logging and manufacturing processes are expected to conform to the
environmental regulations of the country of origin.

Hodder & Stoughton Ltd
338 Euston Road
London NW1 3BH

www.hodder.co.uk

For Phoebe, Alice and Tom

CONTENTS

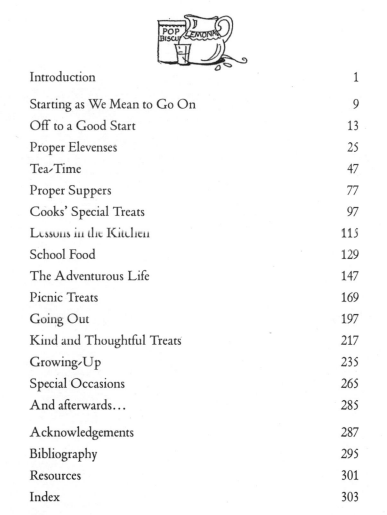

Introduction   1

Starting as We Mean to Go On   9

Off to a Good Start   13

Proper Elevenses   25

Tea-Time   47

Proper Suppers   77

Cooks' Special Treats   97

Lessons in the Kitchen   115

School Food   129

The Adventurous Life   147

Picnic Treats   169

Going Out   197

Kind and Thoughtful Treats   217

Growing-Up   235

Special Occasions   265

And afterwards…   285

Acknowledgements   287

Bibliography   295

Resources   301

Index   303

INTRODUCTION

This book is the result of shared, twin passions: books and foods, reading and eating. It was conceived several years ago during a very English family holiday in Sussex in a restored priory belonging to the Landmark Trust, complete with ruins, rambling garden, walls to climb, places to hide in and plenty of books to read.

One morning, Phoebe and I were sitting in what we called the monks' breakfast room, a semi-open-air room with a long, wooden refectory table and benches, ancient stone carvings, a door-less doorway and lots of little nooks and crannies. The perfect setting, in fact, for a children's story: adventures could be plotted at the table, secret gardens or tunnels might be discovered beyond the walls, and we wouldn't have been surprised if medieval characters had suddenly appeared in front of us.

I was flicking through a Sunday newspaper colour supplement when my eye was caught by a photo of the most delicious-looking macaroon. Phoebe, who was sitting next to me reading yet another Enid Blyton story (she was in a marathon stint of reading the Five Find-Outer books), asked me what it was. When I told her it was a macaroon, she said that although she'd never eaten or seen one, she knew about macaroons because the characters in her Enid Blyton books were often eating them, and could we make them ourselves? By coincidence, this casual conversation came only an hour or two after I'd suggested we make scones and lemonade for afternoon tea and Phoebe had reminded me that these were also favourite treats in Enid Blyton's books.

I began to discern a pattern emerging, so I put down my magazine to pursue this mouth-watering and intriguing line of thought. Together we started to recall and discuss the different foodstuffs and food occasions in children's literature, and out of our collective memory tumbled all sorts of wonderful tea-time treats, suppers, picnics, tuck boxes and parties. In fact, we were so excited that we started to make a list of these foods, and it wasn't long before it occurred to both of us that we were looking at the possibility of a cookery book based on the real, delicious food of classic children's fiction – food which, in fact, most readers only ever consume on the page, and never taste in reality.

How many of us have actually settled down to enjoy cherry cake and cold ginger beer sitting at the top of a cliff or in a secret cove? And how many would like to make and eat the food, even if we can't quite recreate the surroundings? Quite a few, we thought.

That moment in Wilmington Priory with Phoebe crystallised all my thoughts about the closely related pleasures of books and treats; it was as if all my childhood reading and subsequent baking had been an unconscious preparation for writing this book. So it was with a huge sense of excitement and indulgence that I set to work reading and rereading piles of books, researching foods and recipes, and testing and tasting, and testing again until I was happy with the results.

Re-immersing myself in the books of childhood was always going to be a delightful experience. I grew up in the 1960s devouring a wide mix of literature – nineteenth- and twentieth-century classics, contemporary titles, fairy tales, school stories, picture books, biographies, historical novels, many of which have stayed in my imagination ever since. Then, later, this early reading was brought up to date and expanded through reading a huge range of books with Tom, Alice and Phoebe

who, I'm delighted to say, were always eager to listen to a story.

When it came to the baking and cooking, though, there was never a break between my childhood and adulthood; the two have merged seamlessy since my first Milly-Molly-Mandy-style efforts when I was very small. Although I baked regularly for my siblings when I was young, the fact that I was self-taught meant that I had a limited repertoire.

Nevertheless, I was so enthusiastic that I didn't stop to worry about my lack of technique and experience, and simply rushed headlong into baking and making. It was only when I had children and therefore a captive and constantly hungry audience that I acquired more confidence and new skills. Even then, I would have loved a book which told me how to make all the treats in the books that had filled my imagination and inspired me.

Children's literature contains a feast, a banquet, a *menu gastronomique* of treats and lovely foodstuffs. So how to choose what to include and what to leave out? I know there is no accounting for taste, but I have tried to look at, and include, the very best of children's literature, the titles that are most likely to be found on bedroom bookshelves, in libraries and attics. The vast majority of the ones I mention are still read today, and only a handful are (unjustifiably, I feel) out of print.

For a treat to qualify, it had to be real food for humans and it had to be possible to make it in an ordinary home kitchen. There are many fabulous fantasy foods in books but *Cherry Cake and Ginger Beer* is not the book for invented recipes that create foods no one has actually ever tasted in real life. So no Google Buns, I'm afraid, or Roald Dahl-style revolting recipes, or magic foods, or hedgerow cuisine as eaten by Hobbits and Redwall characters.

When it came to the time period to be covered that, too, was straightforward. There is very little in the way of tantalising, delicious-sounding food in children's books published before the later part of the nineteenth-century. Until that point, books tend to be vehicles for improving, religious and moral messages; amusement, entertainment, imagination and food are secondary considerations. So the period I cover begins with books by writers such Louisa May Alcott and Susan Coolidge who are not afraid to include the delightful, everyday details of their characters' lives that appeal directly to children.

As it turns out, and through no preplanning on my part, *Cherry Cake and Ginger Beer* covers more or less a century of children's literature (a century that some people are bound to consider a 'golden age'). This is because I discovered that food and treats in children's literature change dramatically around the same time that sexual intercourse began in 1963, as Philip Larkin puts it in his poem 'Annus Mirabilis'.

It's true; very few books after that date contain the powerfully evocative, real, home-made foods that feature so prominently in ones up to the 1950s. That is not to say that there are not many, many outstanding titles written after this date; it's just that the nature of the food content changes. Novels become grittier, more concerned with realism and specific and social issues, and they begin to reflect the changes that take place in the home, the workplace and the kitchen. With fewer mothers and cooks making traditional cakes and biscuits, food becomes faster, branded, more convenient, and the lavish teas and suppers enjoyed after non-stop adventuring disappear as children's lives become more restricted and guarded.

And what did I leave out? Well, I deliberately excluded picture books in favour of books in which the printed word does the work in the child's imagination. I wanted to include recipes for treats whose appeal and resonance is created by the context in which they are discovered, and which are not simply inspired by an illustration, no matter how colourful or mouth-watering.

When dealing with a series of books by a single writer, I have generally limited myself to the first title, for example *Anne of Green Gables*, *A Bear Called Paddington* and *Little Women*. To my mind, it's as if this first outing conveys the essence of the

character in its best and purest form – like high-quality vanilla extract – so a small amount will give all the flavour you need. A secondary reason is that sequels often contain the same food or foods, which are used as recurring motifs, like Paddington's marmalade sandwiches.

There are, however, a few series in which the food occasions are fresh and new with each book. I'm thinking here of the Milly-Molly-Mandy stories and the Swallows and Amazons novels. And there are series which have such a consistently wonderful and varied food content that each book is a gastronomic treat, as is the case with Enid Blyton.

Some books were omitted even though they fall into the correct time period and categories. These are classics which feature characters and situations that have passed into the collective memory of childhood, and yet when you look closely you find they lack any food substance. *Peter Pan* and *Little Lord Fauntleroy* are two titles that spring to mind; it's as though these characters' other-worldly natures mean they don't require sustenance like ordinary children. And then there's Lewis Carroll's Alice who thinks and talks a great deal about eating and drinking, but only ever eats small portions of magic food, and is plainly disgusted by the lack of decent food and treats at the March Hare's tea party.

Finally, there are many wonderful American and Australian books that are full of delicious foods (enough to fill a companion volume to this one) but I find myself unable to include them here because they are not widely known and read in the United Kingdom.

When it came to arranging the contents of this book, I decided to group the recipes according to food occasion rather than food type. This approach reflects the scenes in which young readers first encounter memorable foodstuffs and treats; indeed it's often the case that the setting is just as important and evocative as the food itself. How else can we explain the irresistible allure of hard-boiled eggs until they are eaten as part of a Famous Five picnic? Or the appeal of marmalade roll until it is served by Mrs Beaver in *The Lion, the Witch and the Wardrobe*?

With its combination of descriptive introductions and tried-and-tested recipes, *Cherry Cake and Ginger Beer* will, I hope, offer reading pleasure as well as inspiration and practical guidance. I like to think that readers will be whisked off to discover (or rediscover) another time and place before being returned to the kitchen and to the joys and pleasures of home baking. If you read the books in your childhood, you will be able to overlay these literary foods with recollections of your own reading and add an extra-special personal seasoning of treasured memories. And if this book encourages anyone, young or old, to read the books and make the treats for the first time, or to experience new literary and gustatory treats, I shall be delighted.

Jane Brocket, March 2008

STARTING AS WE MEAN TO GO ON

Before we begin indulging in treats both fictional and culinary, I think it's important to work up an appetite. Books and cakes, prose and pies, tales and tarts all taste so much better when one's mind and senses are sharpened by a well-earned hunger.

If there is one clear message that runs through all the children's books I have read while preparing this collection of recipes, it's that there should always be a balance between input and output, activity and eating, hunger and consumption.

Eating for the sake of eating is not pleasurable or desirable, and the authors who write best about food are those who understand this.

The most accomplished children's writers also give their readers a break between meals. If you look carefully at well-structured books, you will find that a chapter that features a meal or treat is rarely followed by another chapter containing food. It's as if the writer does not want to spoil the reader's appetite for delicious treats and descriptions, and prefers to make sure he or she is hungry before moving on to the next meal. For a surfeit of indulgences and delicacies is not good in real life or in fiction.

And anyway, there is something quite grotesque about children in books who eat and eat and eat. We know that Billy Bunter is one of the greediest boys in literature, but his lack of self-control is made all the more unpalatable by his habit of stealing other boys' food and eating it in secret. He bypasses many of the pleasurable, civilised aspects of food such preparing and sharing and using knives and forks, and simply gorges on jam straight from the jar.

This is why I prefer reading about food in books where the characters are truly hungry. And it is why I find a description such as this in *The Ragamuffin Mystery* by Enid Blyton so appealing:

"Breakfast was as good as supper had been. Cold ham, boiled eggs, hot toast, home-made marmalade, creamy butter, and scalding hot coffee... Miss Pepper looked at the table with much approval."

It's not just the adjectives that do it (it's amazing how much more prosaic 'ham, eggs, toast, marmalade, butter and coffee' sounds); it's also the fact that you know the children who are about to enjoy this marvellous breakfast are going to spend their day outside swimming, walking, cycling, rowing, bird-watching, climbing trees and apprehending villains. As I am a firm believer in the fact that a healthy hunger is worth cultivating in order to enjoy treats to the full, I'm offering a recipe based on the way it's done in the best children's books.

RECIPE FOR HUNGER

INGREDIENTS:

Beach / hills / garden / park / field / woods / secret island

Outdoor shoes and clothes

Swimming costume and towel

Trampoline

Bicycle

Roller skates, skipping rope, balls

Trees for climbing

Map and compass

Binoculars

Flower / tree / bird reference books (the Observer *books fit nicely in pockets)*

METHOD:

1. In large space, mix adults and children with fresh air.
2. Add outdoor equipment as required and according to season.
3. Allow the ingredients to blend for several hours.
4. When blended, remove from outdoors, and bring inside.
5. Bake or make a treat or two.
6. Feed well, and leave to read good books.

Off To a
Good Start

Breakfast is taken very seriously in children's
books. Writers have no time for those who
skip breakfast or breakfast lightly on the hoof
— why should they? They can't afford to have
their characters fading by mid-morning, their
tummies rumbling and their commitment to the
plot fading rapidly due to a deficit of energy and calories. Even Mary and Colin in
The Secret Garden can't refuse the delicious breakfasts brought to them despite
their plans to starve to death — how else could they cultivate their garden, if not on
porridge and ham and jam and cream and raspberries?

Although the home-cooked breakfasts in books are mostly a variation on a
theme, the focus is on quality as well as quantity, on freshness, wholesomeness, and
lovely combinations of taste and smell and texture, and it it is these qualities that
makes them so appetising. The elements may be ordinary, but when they are written
about with appreciation, they are raised to a new level of deliciousness. Fresh milk,
thick cream and golden butter. Farmhouse honey, home-made jams and marmalades.
New-laid eggs, home-cured bacon, sizzling sausages, little mushrooms and
tureens of porridge with golden syrup. And always plenty of new bread or crisp
toast, steaming coffee or scalding tea.

It must also be remembered that the literature covered in this book is set in a
time when most houses lacked central heating, and children were expected to be
outside and active for most of the day. So hearty breakfasts had to be filling and

energising. In *The Little White Horse* Maria's first breakfast at Moonacre reassures the reader that although she is a fluttery, ethereal child by nature, she is very corporeal when it comes to eating. Her hearty appetite underlines the endearing mix of earthly and unearthly in her character, and the reader knows that Maria has staying power.

"They didn't only have sausages for breakfast. Digweed brought in as well a huge home-cured ham, brown boiled eggs, coffee, tea, new-baked bread, honey, cream with a thick yellow crust on top of it, freshly churned butter, and milk so new it was still warm and frothing. So wide and delicious was the choice that Maria excelled herself in the way of appetite."

It's really very simple to recreate a good literary breakfast as a treat; all you have to do is shop wisely and locally for good ingredients, and make a little extra effort to cook porridge or pancakes or eggs or bacon. The most difficult thing is taking the time to do so and to see a good breakfast as the best way to start the day, even if you don't have an adventure to pursue, a mystery to solve or a secret garden to nurture.

CREAMY PORRIDGE

"The two munched away hard, gazing out of the window. Daffodils danced at the edge of the lawn, and wallflowers shook the scent from their velvet petals. Sunshine flooded the garden and the two children felt happy and excited. The weeks stretched before them – no lessons, no rules – only day after day of sunshine and holidays, enormous meals, ice creams – and Loony, the dog, to take for walks.

'Heavenly,' said Diana."

In a few strokes of the pen, Enid Blyton transports the eager reader to the dining room in *The Rilloby Fair Mystery*. He or she can almost taste the creamy porridge, sausages, toast, marmalade and bread that Roger and Diana are munching, smell the flowers, admire the view and, most important of all, share the tingling, tantalising sense of freedom and the possibility of excitement and intrigue.

But no matter how inviting the outdoor scene, there's an unwritten rule in all good books that you can't run outside on an empty stomach, and Enid Blyton always makes sure both her readers and fictional children venture forth on a sensible, filling breakfast. No skipping this vital meal, and no commercial cereals or sugary drinks. Miss Blyton knows that what you need for fresh spring days in the sunshine is plenty of porridge and plenty of cream. And no stinting on either.

Some people maintain that porridge should only ever be made with water, but I make no apologies for using milk and cream for this is *creamy* porridge – filling and delicious and luxurious, and a great way for everyone in the family to start a spring/winter/autumn day. It's also very easy to make – just don't wander off while it cooks as it can catch and stick to the pan very quickly.

I've given guideline quantities below, but once I know how much milk and oats I need I find the easiest way to measure them out is to find a suitably sized cup and use this each time – the basic rule is to allow two cups of milk to every cup of porridge oats. It's much less bother than weighing out oats on the scales and milk in a jug first thing in the morning. I use a non-stick pan, which ensures that I am not faced with a pan covered in a horrible, gloopy mess after cooking.

Per person:
50 g traditional porridge oats
200 ml milk
Pinch of salt (optional)
Double cream, golden caster sugar or golden syrup, to serve

1. Put the milk and oats into the pan, stir with a wooden spoon and cook gently for 6 minutes, adding a swirl of milk or cream if the porridge gets too thick too quickly – but don't cook it for less than 6 minutes as the oats need to be cooked thoroughly and the milk needs to thicken.
2. Serve with sugar or golden syrup and cream.

Wake-Up-and-Smell the-Bacon Breakfast with Hash Browns

I would much prefer to be told to 'wake and smell the coffee' than 'pay attention to what's going on around you and do something about it'. The phrase is gentle and appealing, rather like the smell of coffee itself. Although it was popularised by the American advice columnist Ann Landers, in the title of her book published in 1996, it would seem that the metaphor was known to E.B.White and Fern, the heroine of *Charlotte's Web*, long before then.

I have noticed that very few children's writers deal with the sense of smell, but *Charlotte's Web* stands out in a generally aroma-free genre. Warm, earthy, farmyardy smells pervade the book, and they draw the reader into the farm, the house and the story, nose in air and sniffing like one of the Bisto kids in the old adverts.

The first chapter begins with some lovely aromas. It is a clever touch to have the farmhouse kitchen smelling mouth-wateringly of bacon just as the young Fern Arable decides to prevent her father killing a small, weak newly born piglet. Having saved Wilbur's bacon, so to speak, she goes back into the house and "the kitchen table was set for breakfast, and the room smelt of coffee, bacon, damp plaster, and wood-smoke from the stove".

And there you are, sitting in a farmhouse in Maine, surrounded by enticing, natural smells, all ready to hear what happens to Wilbur. Will he, or won't he, become just another breakfast dish?

Although I am sure that this story may have put some readers off bacon for ever, it does the opposite to me, and makes me wish I could wake up to the delicious smell of coffee and bacon every day.

It's worth buying best quality, traditionally cured bacon that has come from pigs that have been well looked after; once you have tasted it there is no going back to the plastic-wrapped, anonymous supermarket version. The taste, the texture and, above all, the smell cannot be beaten.

Such excellent bacon turns an ordinary breakfast into a treat. So why not go the whole hog, if you'll pardon the expression, and treat yourself to a wonderful American-style breakfast, the kind that would be enjoyed in a farmhouse in Maine in the 1950s? Add Mate Susan's Scrambled Eggs (page 149), freshly made coffee and the extra flourish of home-made hash browns, cooked in the bacon fat as in the recipe below.

Then simply wake up and smell it all.

Serves 4–6
4 medium potatoes
2–3 tablespoons leftover bacon fat
Plenty of salt and pepper

1. Peel and grate the potatoes.
2. Heat the bacon fat in a large, heavy frying pan.
3. When the fat is hot, tip in the potatoes and spread them to form a layer on the base of the pan, pressing down with a spatula to flatten. Season well with salt and pepper.
4. Cook on a medium heat for 6–8 minutes.
5. Cut the circle in half with the spatula, and turn each half over and season again.
6. Cook for a further 6–8 minutes or until the potatoes are crisp and brown on the bottom.

PURSEY'S COMFORTING
BOILED EGGS

What could be more comforting and consoling than a freshly boiled egg in a knitted cosy, served with bread and butter fingers? This is the small but significant breakfast made by nurse Pursey which tells the sad, orphaned Rachel in *Dancing Shoes* that she is not completely abandoned and unloved.

"There were eggs to follow, nice brown ones, with knitted cosies to keep them warm, in the shape of chicken's heads, and dear little bone spoons to eat them with. Served with them was brown bread and butter.

'Cut the bread and butter into fingers,' Pursey said to Rachel. 'I know it sounds a nursery way, but I've been in nurseries all my life, and I've found that when you are off your food there's nothing like nursery ways for bringing the appetite back.'"

Indeed, there isn't, and Rachel's eyes swim with tears at Pursey's kindness. Finally, she blinks, sees the egg and is surprised. "Somehow it had all been eaten, and so had the bread and butter fingers."

My eyes fill up, too, as I read this. But, I also want to laugh at the lovely, whimsical detail of the chicken egg cosies. It's an immensely cheering moment, one that reaffirms the importance of kind gestures and boiled eggs.

There is something about the wholeness and singleton status of boiled eggs – you can't share them – that makes every self-contained egg a special treat. They are the perfect cheering-up treat for sad or poorly children and world-weary adults alike, and they make the best-ever breakfast in bed. And, personally, I don't believe anyone is too old for soldiers or bread and butter fingers with their boiled eggs.

A BREAKFAST TRAY TO MAKE A CHILD SMILE

Large wooden tray

Napkin

Small spoon

Boiled egg(s) in special egg cup(s)

Soldiers (bread and butter or toast and butter)

Salt and pepper, if liked

Glass of cold milk or iced water

OPTIONAL EXTRAS:

Knitted egg cosies (free patterns can be found on the internet)

Copy of the Beano *or a favourite comic*

Small vase or egg cup with fresh flower(s)

A good book or audio-book – Dancing Shoes *and* Ballet Shoes *are my two Noel Streatfeild favourites*

MA'S PANCAKE MEN

I am a great fan of American-style pancakes. I was converted years ago by a huge stack of the lightest, fluffiest pancakes at Lou Mitchell's Café in Chicago. Ever since then, I have forsworn the large, flat English- and French- style crêpes in favour of the smaller and sweeter American version.

My children have grown up thinking the latter *are* English pancakes, and it's only on Shrove Tuesdays that they realise they are not. We serve them with maple syrup and seasonal fruit, and in the past I used to make what we call 'Barbie' pancakes – tiny dots that can be served to dolls and suchlike. But I had never thought of making pancake men until I reread *Little House in the Big Woods*.

"For breakfast there were pancakes, and Ma made a pancake man for each one of the children. Ma called each one in turn to bring her plate, and each could stand by the stove and watch, while with the spoonful of batter Ma put on the arms and the legs and the head. It was exciting to watch her turn the whole little man over, quickly and carefully on a hot griddle. When it was done, she put it smoking hot on the plate."

What chance do ordinary pancakes stand after you've tasted one of Ma's pancake men?

You can use the recipe below to make Ma's pancake men or simple, round pancakes. Either way, I can guarantee they will be enormously popular with both adults and children. I often serve these pancakes at the weekend; the batter is quick and easy to make and it doesn't need to stand before cooking.

MAKES 8–10 PANCAKE MEN OR 20–24 ROUND PANCAKES

75 g butter, plus extra for greasing

300 ml milk

2 eggs

180 g plain flour

1 tablespoon caster sugar

4 teaspoons baking powder

½ teaspoon salt

Maple syrup and fresh fruit, to serve

Flat frying pan, pancake pan or griddle

1. Put the butter and milk in a small pan and warm over a low heat just long enough to melt the butter. Set aside to cool a little.
2. Lightly beat the eggs in a small bowl, then add the butter and milk mixture. Stir to mix.
3. Put the flour, sugar, baking powder and salt into a large bowl, and stir with a fork to mix. Pour the egg mixture into the flour mixture and stir with a large spoon until the dry ingredients are incorporated – but don't overmix (this doesn't have to be as well mixed as a sponge cake recipe).
4. Heat the pan or griddle and butter it very lightly by running a piece of kitchen paper dipped in a tiny amount of butter over its surface.
5. To make round pancakes, ladle a spoonful of mixture on to the pan for each pancake (it's best to keep them quite small so that they cook evenly) – up to five or so at a time – and cook until the bubbles break on the surface. Flip the pancakes over and cook for another 30 seconds or until the bottoms are lightly browned. Serve immediately.
6. To make a pancake man, make a central body circle, then five smaller circles for

the head, arms and legs. You need to work quickly so that the batter runs and joins together to make a whole that can be turned over. Follow Ma and make only one man at a time otherwise you could end up with some strange pancake creatures. Unless, of course, that is your objective.

7. Serve with maple syrup and fresh fruit such as raspberries, strawberries or blueberries.

PROPER ELEVENSES

'Elevenses' is a quintessentially British ritual and one that I, like Winnie-the-Pooh and Hobbits, am very keen to uphold. I was brought up with elevenses and an appreciation of the moment scheduled halfway between breakfast and lunch for a little sit-down and a reward. Elevenses assumes a certain amount has been accomplished thus far in the day, and is the opportunity to share a light treat, a drink and some companionable chat, preferably about the merits of biscuits or buns or cakes, or some such desultory topic of conversation.

Proper elevenses were easier in the days when there was always someone in the kitchen: a mother, a grandmother or a cook who could conjure up a baked treat by mid-morning. Most of us can't do this on a regular basis, but there is a lot to be said for making the time now and again to put on a pinny and whip up a tray of buns or biscuits. It's not difficult to adapt – think of Paddington Bear all the way from Darkest Peru who embraces this English concept with enthusiasm, or the Famous Five whose internal food-alarm clocks go off every day at 11 a.m.

What you choose to eat and drink should not be too heavy or filling, nor should it be dreary and boring. As you'll see in the following pages, spice buns, warm jam tarts, fresh marmalade buns and gooey macaroons are all perfect candidates for proper elevenses, and there are many other recipes in this book that would make suitable treats to be enjoyed at eleven o'clock.

For more suggestions for elevenses see Mrs Glump's Melt-in-the-Mouth Short-bread (page 74); Mrs Banks' Bribery and Corruption Cocoanut Cakes (page 54); Mary Poppins' Strike-Me-Pink Raspberry Jam Cakes (page 199); Cook's Special Sugar Biscuits (page 230); Pippi Longstocking's Heart-Shaped Swedish Ginger Snaps (page 246); Proper-Meeting Rock Buns (page 239); Camp-Fire Cocoa (page 165); Debby's Jumbles (page 105); Swallows and Amazons Seed Cake (page 154).

AWFULLY GOOD
NEW-MADE BREAD

O ne of my earliest memories is of sitting up in a huge, navy-blue pram, eating freshly baked bread from a white paper bag which had been half-hidden underneath my blankets. It was mid-morning, I'd just been taken to the baker's by my Nana and she indulged my desire to tear pieces from the loaf and eat them while they were still warm. When we arrived home, though, my mum disapproved deeply of my elevenses. The result is that, to this day, I still get an illicit thrill from eating bread that has just come straight out of the oven. Indeed, I now time my bread-baking to allow for maximum warm bread-eating, and have shamelessly encouraged my children to eat home-made bread as soon as it's cool enough to slice.

So I empathise fully with Dick (the character with the most finely tuned gastronomic tendencies in the Famous Five stories) when the children buy six enormous loaves to take with them when they abscond in *Five Run Away Together* and he finds he simply can't resist the temptation to eat some straightaway.

"'Doesn't that new-made bread smell awfully good?' said Dick, feeling very hungry as usual. 'Can we just grab a bit, do you think?'

'Yes, let's,' said George. So they broke off bits of the warm brown crust...and chewed the delicious new-made bread."

I think every child would like to enjoy bread like this, especially after reading about it in many of Enid Blyton's books where it is invariably called 'new bread' or 'new-made bread' – so much more appetising than just 'bread'. So here's a very simple, reliable recipe that makes an awfully good loaf, and which should be made so it's ready to eat around eleven o'clock, just as tummies are beginning to rumble.

MAKES 1 LARGE LOAF
500 g strong flour
15 g fresh yeast or 1 dessertspoon dried yeast
1 teaspoon caster sugar or runny honey
500 ml lukewarm water
3 teaspoons sea salt
Oil, for greasing

Baking tray or 900 g loaf tin, oiled

1. Measure the flour into a large mixing bowl.
2. Put the yeast and caster sugar or honey in a small bowl, add the lukewarm water and stir to mix. Add 2 tablespoons of the flour and mix again. Leave for 20 minutes until there is a frothy, foamy layer on the surface of the liquid, which indicates the yeast is alive and well. If there is no bubbling, the yeast is dead and you will need to start again with a new batch of yeast.
3. Stir the salt into the flour, make a well in the centre and pour in the liquid. If the mix seems very dry add a little more water. With one hand work the mix briefly until it comes together and leave for a minute or so to let the flour absorb the water.
4. Now turn the dough out on to a floured work surface. Be careful not to use too much flour here as this will stiffen the dough. I like to work with a sticky dough and flour it little and often, but others prefer to handle a firmer, drier dough.
5. Knead for 5–8 minutes until the texture of the dough changes and it becomes smooth and elastic.
6. Form the dough into a ball. Lightly oil the bowl and return the dough to the bowl. Cover with clingfilm or a damp tea towel and leave in a warm place until the dough has doubled in size (this can take 1–2 hours depending on conditions on the day). It is also possible to put the dough in the fridge to rise

slowly, in which case allow 4–6 hours or leave overnight.

7. When the dough has risen, punch it down – that is, gently deflate it with a floured hand. Turn it on to a floured work surface and knead until smooth, about 2–3 minutes, then place it in the loaf tin or shape it into a round and place it on the baking tray. Cover with oiled clingfilm and leave to rise again for about an hour.

8. While the bread is rising preheat the oven to 200°C/Gas Mark 6.

9. Remove the clingfilm and bake for 30–40 minutes until risen and golden. The best way to make sure bread is done is to take it out of the oven for a moment, remove it from its tin if necessary, and tap it on its underside. If there is a hollow sound it is cooked, if not, carry on baking.

10. Remove and transfer the loaf to a wire cooling rack. Do not expect it to stay there for long.

RED KITCHEN JAM TARTS

Picture this. Three children are sitting down to a mid-morning feast in the huge, old kitchen of a sunny farmhouse. The floor is tiled with old red bricks, so clean that it seems a shame to tread on them. A cheerful red fire burns at one end. Bright red geraniums are flowering on the windowsill, and there are cups and saucers with a bright red pattern on the dresser.

Out of a capacious larder comes Mrs Timbles, a round, beaming farmer's wife, whose face is shining like a large, polished red apple. She is carrying ginger buns and jam tarts that are so full of home-made jam it runs over, and a large jug of nettle beer.

No wonder the humble jam tart takes on a mythical status when presented thus. I can't think of many other food settings that are so lovingly described and imagined – and which coordinate so beautifully with the food being eaten. The little touches of red – Mrs Timbles' face, the tiles, the fire, the flowers and the crockery – all complement the undoubtedly red jam tarts.

As Enid Blyton so obviously understands in *The Treasure Hunters*, home-made jam tarts are the taste of a real, warm, welcoming, hospitable kitchen. They evoke childhood memories of baking with a mother or grandmother and handling soft pastry and sticky red jam. They are simple, homely treats: sweet, colourful, deliciously melting and fruity. The only downside is that you may not have the kitchen to match; but, then again, as thousands of wishful readers have done before, you can always imagine yourself into Mrs Timbles'.

MAKES 16–18 JAM TARTS
180 g plain flour
60 g icing sugar
120 g butter
2 egg yolks or 1 egg yolk plus 2 teaspoons cold water
1 x 340 g jar raspberry or strawberry jam

2 bun trays

1. Make the pastry well in advance so that it has time to chill and rest in the fridge. Sift the flour and icing sugar into a bowl. Quickly rub in the butter then add enough liquid to make the pastry come together (use a little extra water if necessary, but try to be as sparing as possible). Shape into a flattish, hamburger-shaped disc, place in a polythene bag and chill in the fridge for at least an hour.

2. When you are ready to make the jam tarts, preheat the oven to 200°C/Gas Mark 6.

3. Roll out the pastry on a floured surface. Make 16–18 rounds with a pastry cutter, place the circles in the bun trays and chill in the fridge for a minimum of 30 minutes.

4. When you are ready to bake the tarts, remove the bun trays from fridge and spoon a good teaspoon of your chosen jam on to the centre of each pastry circle. Don't be mean, but make sure you don't overfill the circles as the jam will bubble and rise during baking. You want it to run over just a little.

5. Bake in the oven for 12–15 minutes, checking towards the end of this time that the tarts are not burning. When the edges are turning gold, remove from the oven. Leave the tarts in their bun trays on a wire rack to cool, then turn out.

Pursey's Surprise Hot Cross Buns

I had a teacher at junior school who used to boom at all the nine-year-olds in her class, usually apropos some inappropriate classroom activity, that 'there is a time and a place for everything'. I wasn't always convinced – some subversive laughter often lightened our lessons – but now that I am older and wiser I have a better idea of what she meant. And I found the perfect illustration of this concept in *Dancing Shoes* by Noel Streatfeild.

It's Good Friday. Rachel, Hilary and Pursey have left the house early to take a train to Sussex to pick primroses.

"It was a truly superb wood. The primroses made a yellow carpet, with a pattern of dog violets and wood anemones running through them. In spite of Easter being late that year, though some of the trees had leaves, there were still some buds which had an out-any-minute-now look. So many birds were singing they might have been rehearsing for a bird concert."

This magical spot becomes one of those 'time and place' moments for Rachel, who is grieving for her mother. She picks and picks, and finds herself surprised that the world still has lovely things in it, such as primroses and birds' nests, and she's even more surprised to discover that she has enough room for another of the hot cross buns that Pursey has thoughtfully brought with them to sustain them until lunchtime.

These days it is hard to recreate the special 'time and place' quality of Good Friday. Hot cross buns are available all year round in supermarkets, and it is not a good idea to pick wild primroses. But if you have never eaten home-made hot cross buns you, too, are in for surprise because they are immeasurably better than anything you can buy in the shops.

Of course, there is nothing to say that hot cross buns without the cross cannot be enjoyed all year round. But even though I often think about making them at other times, there is something very enjoyable about a once-a-year treat, and going through all the processes of kneading, shaping, piping the crosses, baking and then adding the sticky syrup glaze. A tray of just-cooked hot cross buns is a beautiful sight – like a glowing, modernist, stained-glass window.

So choose Good Friday or a bright spring day, make hot cross buns for elevenses, pick daffodils, look for (and leave) clumps of primroses on green banks or in dappled woods, and enjoy the time and the place.

I have tried several hot cross bun recipes and the one below gives by far the best results. It is adapted from the recipe in *Baking with Passion* by Dan Lepard and, although it may seem a little more demanding than the other bun recipes in this book, it is undoubtedly worth the effort. If you leave the crosses off, you have old-fashioned spice buns.

MAKES 20–24 HOT CROSS BUNS

670 g strong white flour

25 g skimmed milk powder

1 teaspoon ground mixed spice

½ nutmeg, grated

15 g salt

100 g caster sugar

85 g soft butter

1 egg

75 g sultanas

75 g raisins

50 g dried mixed peel

Oil, for greasing

FOR THE SPONGE:

200 g strong white flour
15 g fresh yeast or 1 dessertspoon dried yeast
1 teaspoon runny honey or sugar
230 ml lukewarm water

FOR THE CROSSES:

4 tablespoons plain flour
1 tablespoon caster sugar

FOR THE GLAZE:

3 tablespoons sugar

1 large or 2 medium baking trays, lined with baking parchment

1. First make a sponge. Weigh the flour into a large mixing bowl and add the yeast, honey or sugar and lukewarm water. Whisk well to mix, cover with clingfilm and leave for 1½ –2 hours until risen and bubbly on the surface.
2. Now make the dough. Put the flour in a large bowl and add the skimmed milk powder, mixed spice, nutmeg, salt, sugar, butter, egg, 230 ml water and the sponge. With one hand bring the mixture together into a sticky dough.
3. Mix for 5 minutes with an electric mixer, or turn out on to a floured surface and knead for 5 minutes until the dough feels smooth and elastic.
4. Add the dried fruit and peel and knead in (this can be difficult at first when mixing by hand, but the fruit does eventually adhere).
5. Lightly grease the bowl with oil, form the dough into a ball and return it to the bowl. Cover with clingfilm and leave to rise in a warm place for 1½ –2 hours until

the dough has doubled in size.

6. Punch the dough down, that is, gently deflate it with a floured fist. Turn it out and divide it into equal pieces by weighing them on scales (I find 90-g balls make generous hot cross buns) then roll each piece into a ball. Arrange the balls on the tray(s) so that they are almost, but not quite, touching. Cover with clingfilm or a damp tea towel and leave to rise in a warm place for 45 minutes while you preheat the oven to 180°C/Gas Mark 6.

7. While the buns are rising, make the paste for the crosses. Mix the flour and sugar with enough water to make a stiff paste and put this into a piping bag with a medium-size plain nozzle. A large empty plastic syringe makes an excellent alternative to a piping bag.

8. When the buns have risen, make a cross on the top of each one with a very sharp knife then pipe some of the paste into the indentation.

9. Bake for 30–40 minutes or until the buns are golden and browning round the edges, and sound hollow when tapped on the base.

10. Place the tray(s) on a wire rack and glaze the buns. To make the glaze, dissolve the sugar in 3 tablespoons water and bring to the boil. Boil for 10 seconds then remove from heat and brush over the buns. These buns are most delicious when warm and fresh.

PADDINGTON BEAR'S FAVOURITE MARMALADE BUNS

I know someone who used to say that he kept his morals in a suitcase under his bed. Well, Paddington Bear not only keeps his morals with him at all times, he also carries his suitcase wherever he goes, and always makes sure it contains a little something to eat in case of unplanned hunger.

Paddington is one of an illustrious line of hungry bears in children's literature and many children are first introduced to marmalade by his passion for it. One of the joys of coming to London from Darkest Peru, where marmalade is scarce and regarded as a special treat is that he is allowed by the generous and accommodating Brown family to have marmalade every day (and honey on Sundays). So Paddington Bear is able to buy his favourite marmalade buns with his pocket money, take marmalade sandwiches with him to the theatre and bring a jar of marmalade to the seaside.

While marmalade sandwiches may be too much of a good thing for younger palates, marmalade buns are more gently orangey. So here is a recipe for marmalade buns that would appeal to Paddington Bear. The kind of bun he might enjoy for elevenses with his good friend Mr Gruber, who keeps an antique shop on Portobello Road in London: "Mr Gruber usually had a bun and a cup of cocoa in the morning for what he called 'elevenses', and he had taken to sharing it with Paddington. 'There's nothing like a chat over a bun and cocoa,' he used to say, and Paddington, who liked all three, agreed with him – even though the cocoa did make his whiskers go a funny colour."

How wonderfully cosy-sounding and utterly irresistible.

The recipe below is very flexible and can be made as buns (small sponge cakes) or a single cake in a loaf tin. I ice my buns/cake with a simple icing made with icing sugar and fresh orange juice, but they are also delicious without icing – and make far less mess in suitcases. They go just as well with tea, coffee and orange squash as they do with cocoa and it's worth reinstating elevenses simply as an excuse to eat them. They are also the perfect accompaniment to a reading-aloud session of favourite Paddington Bear stories.

MAKES 1 LARGE CAKE OR 12 SMALL BUNS
175 g butter
175 g soft brown sugar
3 eggs
Grated zest of 1 orange (unwaxed)
Juice of ½ orange
2 rounded tablespoons thin-cut marmalade
175 g self-raising flour

FOR THE ICING:
200 g icing sugar
Juice of 1 orange
Orange food-colouring paste (optional)

1 12-bun tray and 12 paper cases or 1 large (25 x 11 x 7 cm) loaf tin, greased with butter and lined with baking parchment

1. Preheat the oven to 180°C/Gas Mark 4. Place the paper cases, if using, in the bun tin.
2. In a mixing bowl, beat the butter and sugar until light and fluffy. Add the eggs one by one until fully incorporated into the mix. Add the orange zest, orange juice and marmalade and stir in thoroughly.
3. Add the flour and fold in gently with a large metal spoon.
4. Divide the mix equally between the paper cases and place them in the bun tray or spoon it into the loaf tin.
5. If you are making one cake, bake for 40–50 minutes, but check after 35 minutes. Use a metal skewer or sharp knife to test for doneness – insert it in the cake and if any trace of uncooked mixture comes out on the skewer or knife the cake is not fully cooked. Return it to the oven and bake until the knife or skewer comes out clean. If you find your cake is browning a little too quickly, place a sheet of foil on top of the cake to prevent it burning.
6. If you are making a dozen small buns they will need approximately 20 minutes baking time.
7. Transfer the tin(s) to a wire rack and leave the buns/cake to cool. Do not begin to ice them until they are completely cold.
8. To make the icing, sift the icing sugar into a bowl and add half the orange juice and a tiny amount of orange food-colouring paste, if using, and mix. Add as much juice as it takes to make the icing thick and glossy and spread the icing over the buns/cake.

MELBOURNE MORNING-
TEA WALNUT CAKE

When I asked the readers of my blog yarnstorm for suggestions for classic Australian children's books, I was overwhelmed by the warm, enthusiastic response and the number of titles that clearly brought back fond memories. Of all the books mentioned, I was most intrigued by the Billabong stories, a series of fifteen books written between 1910 and 1942 by Mary Grant Bruce. They promote the ideals of Australian mateship and hard work, are clean, wholesome and pleasant (the author refused to include love interest), and are peopled with extremely likeable characters. And each tale is embellished with beautiful descriptions of Australia's brilliant natural landscapes and the lovingly imagined vegetable and flower gardens at Billanbong.

The leading character is the motherless Norah Linton, an appealing, haphazardly educated tomboy who loves the outdoor life but who at the age of eleven can cook like a dream and knit socks and shawls (but refuses to sew). I decided Norah was my kind of heroine when I read *Mates at Billabong*; at one point she sits happily in the kitchen, a dab of flour on her nose, encased in a voluminous white apron, writing a letter to her brother while watching a cake in the oven.

Norah stars in all the books, but the one I enjoyed the most was one that, ironically, gives a revealing glimpse of Britain and British baking during, and after, the First World War from an Australian point of view. In *Back to Billabong* Norah and her father have spent the war years in England, and return to Australia with her brother Jim and friend Wally. They sail into Melbourne and one of the very first things their party does is partake of "morning tea – that time-honoured institution of Australia" with Aunt Jean. Their appreciation of this taste of home, the feast after the famine, makes you realise that it wasn't only during the Second World War that treats were scarce:

"The last four years in England had fairly broken people into plain living; dainties and luxuries had disappeared so completely from the table that every one had ceased to think about them. Therefore, the Linton party blinked in amazement at the details of what to Melbourne was a very ordinary tea...

'Cakes!' said Wally, faintly. 'Jean, you might catch me if I swoon.'"

But he doesn't, and they all recover sufficiently to enjoy enormous slices of cake filled with thick layers of real cream, cake made with real butter and eggs (not substitutes) and proper sugar without "queer stuff like plaster of paris", cakes which aren't dry and crumbly and which don't fall apart when touched. This is because they are made with flour containing gluten whereas, as Norah explains, in England flour is gluten-free because the gluten is extracted to use in munitions. She turns gratefully to the walnut cake: "It's making me tremble even to look at it."

So here is a recipe for a walnut cake that celebrates, and reminds us of, all the good, real things that go into a fine treat: flour with gluten, fresh eggs, creamy butter and unadulterated sugar. It can be enjoyed with morning tea, afternoon tea or whenever you feel the need to count your blessings.

MAKES 1 MEDIUM CAKE (SERVES 8)

70 g walnuts	*190 g self-raising flour*
180 g soft brown sugar	*½ teaspoon baking powder*
180 g soft butter	*8–10 walnut halves for decoration*
3 eggs	
2 teaspoons instant coffee	
2 teaspoons boiling water	

FOR THE FILLING:

150 g icing sugar

60 g butter, softened

2 teaspoons instant coffee granules

2 teaspoons boiling water

FOR THE ICING:

200 g icing sugar

1–2 teaspoons instant coffee granules

1–2 teaspoons boiling water

2 18-cm round cake tins, greased with butter and lined with baking parchment

1. Preheat the oven to 180°C/Gas Mark 4.
2. Chop the walnuts into small pieces.
3. In a large mixing bowl, cream the sugar and butter until pale and fluffy. Add the eggs one at a time and mix in thoroughly after each addition.
4. Put the instant coffee and boiling water in a small container (an egg cup is ideal) and mix until the granules are fully dissolved.
5. Sift the flour and baking powder into the bowl, pour in the concentrated coffee, add the chopped walnuts and fold in gently with a large metal spoon.
6. Divide the mixture evenly between the cake tins and bake for 20–25 minutes until the cakes are golden brown and springy, and a metal skewer or sharp knife inserted in one of them comes out clean..
7. Leave the cakes in their tins on a wire rack to cool completely, then turn them out and make the filling and topping.
8. To make the filling, sift the icing sugar into a bowl and add the butter. Mix the coffee and boiling water as in Step 4 and pour into the bowl. Mix together with a knife, gradually adding more water if necessary, until you have a smooth, light and spreadable butter cream.
9. Spread the filling over one of the cakes, and place the second cake on top.
10. To make the icing, sift the icing sugar into a bowl. Make the concentrated coffee as in Step 4 (use 1–2 teaspoons water according to taste – you can always add

more as you go along, but the granules must be dissolved first or you will have little dark flecks in the icing). Add this and about 2 tablespoons water to the icing sugar and mix well. Add more water/coffee concentrate sparingly if necessary and according to taste. The icing should be thick and glossy, and not too runny.

11. Spread the icing over the top of the cake and place the walnut halves around the edge for decoration.

It wouldn't be fair to leave Norah without adding this short, delightful postscript:

When the Linton party finally return to Billabong after five years in England, Mrs Brown, the kind, thoughtful housekeeper, not only plies Wally with his favourite pikelets, but also makes a celebratory cake for Norah.

"'An' I've got your fav'rite sponge cake, Miss Norah – ten aigs in it!'

'Ten!' said Norah. 'Doesn't it make you feel light-headed to think of putting ten eggs in one cake again?'

'An' why not?' sniffed Brownie."

And she does because she can.

FRESH AND GOOEY MACAROONS

Macaroons are at the heart of this book; they are where it all started. It was while Phoebe and I were enjoying our elevenses in an ancient priory build-ing that we stumbled upon the idea of closing the gap between reading about food and actually tasting it. Phoebe was engrossed in a Five Find-Outer book by Enid Blyton (the series that stars Fatty who adores macaroons) and I was looking at a magazine. When I came across a glorious photo of a macaroon I pointed it out to Phoebe who exclaimed that she'd been wondering what macaroons were. And so the idea of a cookery book based on food in children's literature was born.

Macaroons pop up time and again in fictional picnics and teas. But I particu-larly like the idea of macaroons for elevenses as they can be consumed without slow-ing one down for the rest of the morning – something that Julian, Dick, Anne and George understand perfectly.

In *Five On Finniston Farm*, the children spend a morning rushing around the farm and building up a stupendous appetite, then go into the village for buns and milk at the dairy. To their delight, they discover that the proprietor has just made a batch of macaroons "all gooey and fresh". Dick (who, I feel sure, grows up to be either a chef or a cookery writer) speaks for them all:

"'Now how did you guess that we are all very partial to macaroons?' said Dick… 'We'll have a plateful, please.'

'What, a whole plateful?' exclaimed Janie. 'But there's about twenty on a plate!' 'Just about right,' said Dick."

When they have cleared the dairy of macaroons, much to the amazement of

Janie's mother who can't believe they have eaten nearly two dozen macaroons and five ice creams, Julian – ever the charmer – says, "*Most* delicious macaroons they were!"

And off they go to find another adventure before lunch.

This recipe makes the traditional English macaroon. It is not the chic French type that comes in exquisite flavours with sophisticated fillings, but the simple almond version that would have been available in deepest, leafy England in the 1940s and 1950s. This recipe makes disc-like confections that are pearly and crisp on the outside and soft, chewy and gooey on the inside.

You will need to use a Teflon sheet or rice paper to line your baking tray; macaroons have a tendency to stick tightly to greaseproof paper, baking parchment and baking trays.

MAKES 12–15 MACAROONS

2 egg whites

200 g icing sugar

200 g ground almonds

A few drops of almond essence

(optional)

Baking tray, lined with a Teflon sheet or rice paper

1. Preheat the oven to 160°C/Gas Mark 3.
2. Put the egg whites in a large bowl and whisk until soft peaks form.
3. Sift the icing sugar over the egg whites, add the ground almonds and the almond essence, if using, and mix gently to a firm paste with a large spoon.
4. Spoon or pipe the paste into rounds on the baking tray, leaving space in between the rounds for each macaroon to spread during cooking.
5. Bake for 20 minutes until the macaroons are just beginning to turn colour. Don't overcook them, though, as they need to be chewy in the middle.
6. Transfer the tray to a wire rack and leave the macaroons to cool. Eat while fresh and gooey.

TEA-TIME

Tea time is a lovely time, whatever time of day you prefer to enjoy it. It's ironic that just as tea (as in a mid- to late-afternoon snack or meal) is in danger of falling into disuse, discussions concerning its timing, etiquette and contents are becoming ever more heated. In fact, you only have to go back to children's classics to see that tea-time is what you make of it, a wonderfully flexible treat that can be enjoyed in the kitchen, drawing room, nursery or outside in the garden, on the beach, up hills and down by lakes, at a time to suit you. It can be an opportunity to entertain or to eat informally, to get out the best china or to use everyday plates and mugs.

Tea time is the perfect time for a baked treat. It's ideal for energetic children who need to be given something tasty and satisfying to keep them going until the evening, and it's the best time of all for bakers to be making cakes and breads and biscuits. As for grown-ups, tea-time is an indulgence worth reviving at weekends or during holidays; there's nothing like a slice of cherry cake, a hot, buttered muffin or a piece of shortbread in the late afternoon to make everything seem all right with the world.

Perhaps it would help to be reminded of those lovely descriptions of tea-time treats in books? Consider this mouth-watering word picture:

"'What a spread!'

"It certainly was. It wasn't an ordinary afternoon-tea, it was a high-tea. A fresh ham, glistening pink. A veal-and-ham pie smothered in parsley, like the ham. Yellow butter in glass dishes. A blue jug of yellow cream. Honey. Home-made strawberry jam. Hot scones. A large fruit cake as black as a plum pudding inside. Egg sandwiches. Tea, cocoa and creamy milk."

This is prose worthy of a fine food writer who revels in the creation and then the written evocation of fresh, simple, home-made food, and lots of it. As I read, I am transported to a cosy, homely kitchen table with pots of geraniums on the window sill, a red-and-white checked tablecloth, a warm oven and a smiling hostess. I picture this beautiful still-life of food, colours, shapes and textures and can feel myself getting hungry. I am as ready to tuck in with gusto as Philip, Jack, Dinah and Lucy-Ann. This is Enid Blyton in *The Circus of Adventure* (1952) at her gastronomic finest.

I hope that excerpts like this and the recipes that follow in this section will inspire and encourage you to reinstate tea-time, too.

For more recipes suitable for afternoon tea see: Mary Poppins' Strike-Me-Pink Raspberry Jam Cakes (page 199); Red Kitchen Jam Tarts (page 30); Fresh and Gooey Macaroons (page 44); Mrs Corry's Gilt Gingerbread (page 202); Just Coconut Kisses (page 210); St Clare's Éclair s (page 205); Loveday's Marriage Proposal Parkin (page 270); Marmaduke Scarlet's Saffron Cake (page 102); Mrs Persimmon's Crumpets (page 267); Pippi Longstocking's Heart-Shaped Swedish Ginger Snaps (page 246); Proper-Meeting Rock Buns (page 239); Debby's Jumbles (page 105); Smashing Match Tea Jammy Buns (page 131); Easy-Peasy Lemonade (page 190); Camp-Fire Cocoa (page 165); Jeremy and Jemima's More-Jam-Than-Puff Jam Puffs (page 185); Swallows and Amazons Seed Cake (page 154); Voyages of Discovery Bunloaf (page 159).

DELICIOUS STEWED FRUIT

I have never come across a better explanation of how tea-time works than the one in *Henrietta's House* by Elizabeth Goudge. It comes from the pen of someone who clearly gave food and eating a great deal of thought; Elizabeth Goudge's books are full of amazing descriptions of kitchens, meals, cooking and treats, and this whimsical discussion of the concept of tea-time is typical of her delight in matters gastronomic.

Young Henrietta lives in an attractively extended bohemian family arrangement, but dreams of having a house in which they can all live together. The story of how her wish comes to be granted takes place over the course of a single day, and is made up of a series of magical, almost fairy-tale, interludes, after which all the various characters come together for tea.

Henrietta and Mrs Jameson are making last-minute preparations for this tea and when it is clear that the guests are going to be late, Henrietta asks, "at what time does tea become high tea?" Mrs Jameson's reply contains the wisdom of great experience:

"At about six o' clock I think, dear… One adds cold ham then, you know, and then as time goes on the tea gets higher and higher and one adds ginger wine and damson cheese and stewed fruit, and sardines if you have any. And then after eight o' clock it isn't high tea any more, but supper, and you can fry bacon and eggs."

Tea is also a movable feast; as it gets higher it also changes location. Mrs Jameson explains: "When it gets to ham it moves to the dining-room, you know, for no one ever eats ham in a drawing-room" and then it can even move from the dining-room to the kitchen "but only after midnight, when the servants are in bed and… one adds cocoa to all the other things."

And off they go to stew some rosy apples.

So there you are. Everything you wanted to know about tea-time, but were afraid to ask.

As I read this wonderful scene, it occurred to me that stewed fruit has somehow become greatly overlooked and despised. Children today are happy to eat something in a plastic pot labelled 'compote' yet would probably turn their noses up at good, old-fashioned, home-made stewed fruit. This is a great shame, as stewed fruit need not be pulpy, bland and predictable; when it is made with good ingredients, and not overcooked, it can be a sweetly delicious partner for custard, cream, ice cream, sponges, pancakes, cheesecakes and all sorts of breakfast foods. Not to mention tea, at any time.

It's easy enough to adapt this recipe for stewed plums to suit the type and quantity of fruit you have or the number of people eating.

SERVES 6–8

1 kg fresh, ripe (but not over-ripe) plums
200–250 g caster sugar or light soft brown sugar
1 vanilla pod or 4–5 cloves (optional)
Custard, cream or ice cream, to serve (optional)

1. Wash the plums if necessary. Slice them in half and remove the stones.
2. Place the plums in a large pan and add about 200 g of the sugar (you can add more if necessary once you have tasted the cooking juice). Stewing fruit is all about personal taste and how sweet you like your fruit to be, so there is no hard and fast rule about sugar quantities.
2. Put in the vanilla pod or cloves, if using.
3. Now add a tiny dash of water so that the base of the pan is covered. The plums will produce liquid as they cook.

4. Cook very gently over a low heat until the plums are soft but not too collapsed. I prefer stewed fruit with a vestige of its original shape, so I tend to remove it from the heat sooner rather than later. Plums take about 8–12 minutes to stew nicely. Stir only if necessary, to avoid breaking them up too much. Shaking the pan gently often works better than stirring.

5. Taste as the plums cook and add more sugar as necessary.

6. Allow to cool a little before serving.

7. Serve warm or cold, with or without extras such as custard or cream or ice cream.

MORE FRUITS AND FLAVOURS

There are many fruits that develop delicious flavours when stewed. The list includes: rhubarb, cherries, apricots, peaches, gooseberries, greengages, blackberries, apples and pears. Each requires a different amount of sugar depending on sweetness and personal taste. There is nothing to stop you adding various flavourings or experimenting with liquids other than water, such as brandy, rum, wine or flavoured spirits such as crème de cassis or crème de framboise.

- Adjust cooking times according to the level of stewing you require. Some fruits cook faster than others.
- Apples go brilliantly with a stick of cinnamon or a good grating of nutmeg or a few cloves.
- Pears halved or quartered and cooked gently in port or red wine with some lemon zest or a vanilla pod make a lovely tea-time treat.
- Try stewing rhubarb with orange (the grated zest of an unwaxed orange) or ginger (a little chopped, fresh ginger or half a teaspoon of ground ginger).
- Combinations of fruit also work well. Summer fruits such as redcurrants, blackcurrants and blackberries can be cooked together with fine results.

MR TUMNUS' TOASTY TEA

I could, and did, look for hours at Pauline Bayne's original illustrations for *The Lion, the Witch and the Wardrobe*. A poor illustrator can distract from or even distort the text, whereas a successful one enhances our reading; and Pauline Baynes pulls off such an amazing feat of envisaging Narnia that I, and I'm sure many other people, could never now imagine it any other way.

Just look at the details here. The small, crowded but neat room, the softly glowing light emanating from the lamp, the large kettle by the fire. The dresser filled with reassuringly ordinary crockery, teapots and tureens to suggest someone who enjoys cooking and eating, the full bookshelves of a keen reader. The little eggs in egg cups on the floor, the comfy armchairs, the table set with tea things and a rather splendid-looking "sugar-topped cake". And, above all, a generously large, blazing fire for making toast.

Because, as Lucy discovers, tea with Mr Tumnus, is all about toast:

"And really it was a wonderful tea. There was a nice brown egg, lightly boiled, for each of them, and then sardines on toast, then buttered toast and then toast with honey."

As Mr Tumnus knows, the comfort value of toast should never be overlooked. It is simple and tasty, and custom can never stale its infinite variety. It is also cheap and easy to prepare, which makes it perfect for a cosy tea in a bookish cave. How sharply this snug, Three Toast Tea contrasts with Edmund's solitary, selfish, gorging on Turkish delight outside in the snow and ice.

Of course, Mr Tumnus' tea is meant to be a kidnap trap so that he can bring Lucy to the Queen, but the toast thaws his intentions and he enjoys meeting her so much that he confesses and lets her go. She saves herself by being kind and friendly and trusting, passes the toast test and goes free, whereas Edmund fails the Turkish

delight test and is thus trapped by his own greed.

The trick with something as simple as toast is to use really good ingredients: good bread, good butter, good toppings.

All the following can be made in front of a fire – no need for a kitchen or a grill. So they are just right for students, campers and centaurs.

Sardines on toast: 1 tin (approximately 125 g) of good-quality Mediterranean sardines in olive oil, drained, should cover two slices of thick, white, buttered toast.

Buttered toast: I am a self-confessed butter snob and I like to be able to taste the butter on my toast, so I use the delicious salted Bridel from France.

Honey and toast: I adore looking at all the different types of honey with their gloriously evocative names and have always liked the idea of honey on toast. But, and this is a terrible handicap for someone who enjoys reading about food in children's literature as much as I do, I don't actually like the taste of honey. Having read so much about it, though, I feel I should include it as a classic toast combination.

Cheese on toast: My children love uncooked cheese on toast. If you slice a firm cheese such as Red Leicester, Cheddar, old Gouda or Emmental very thinly and place it on hot, buttered toast and the cheese will melt just enough to be soft and warm.

MRS BANKS' BRIBERY
AND CORRUPTION
COCOANUT CAKES

In the opening chapter of *Mary Poppins Comes Back*, Mrs Banks is at her wits'
end. Ever since Mary Poppins left without a "Word of Warning", everything is
wrong. The water's too hot, the coffee's too cold, nursery nurses have come and gone
in quick succession, and now it looks like even Mr Banks has left for good. Ellen, the
maid, has taken to her bed with a 'broken leg' and the children's behaviour in the
nursery has descended into anarchy. So Mrs Banks does what any sensible mother
would do and sends all four children out to the park until tea-time with the bribe of
something nice to eat: "... if you will go quietly and be good children there will be
cocoanut [sic] cakes for tea."

And, like good children who know when they have the upper hand, they go
off to the park to fly Michael's kite. Except the kite changes and in its place dances
a familiar figure; it is, of course, Mary Poppins who has come back.

In the blink of an eye because "as usual, everything that Mary Poppins did had
the speed of electricity", order, peace and harmony are restored in the Banks'
household. But the downside is that when Jane and Michael come to eat their
cocoanut cakes they do so in super-quick time, which is no doubt a Poppinish form
of retribution for letting themselves be corrupted by a sweet treat.

It's a shame that all things coconutty are seen as slightly passé these days, as
coconut gives a lovely flavour and dampness to sponge cake. Plus, I think all children
should experience the pleasure of idly picking little flecks of coconut flesh out of

their teeth after eating a cake or two.

If possible, used shredded coconut rather than desiccated coconut as it is sweeter and softer.

MAKES 12 COCONUT CAKES
125 g soft butter
125 g caster sugar
2 eggs
100 g self-raising flour

½ teaspoon baking powder
50 g shredded or desiccated coconut
2 tablespoons milk
Silver balls or coconut-flavoured jelly beans, to decorate (optional)

FOR THE TOPPING:
30 g soft butter
150 g icing sugar

30 g shredded or desiccated coconut
2–3 dessertspoons milk

12-hole bun tray and 12 paper cases
1. Preheat the oven to 180°C/Gas Mark 4 and place the paper cases in the bun tray.
2. In a large mixing bowl, cream the butter and sugar until pale and fluffy.
3. Beat in the eggs.
4. Sift the flour and baking powder over the mix, add the coconut and milk and fold in gently with a large metal spoon.
5. Divide the mix equally between the paper cases and bake for 15–20 minutes until the cakes are golden and their centres feel springy.
6. Leave the cakes in the bun tray on a wire rack until completely cold.
7. To make the topping, cream together the butter, icing sugar and coconut, adding enough milk to make the mixture soft. Spread on top of the cakes.
8. A few silver balls or coconut-flavoured jelly beans on top of each cake may act as added incentives to good behaviour.

Milly-Molly-Mandy's
Muffin Man Muffins

Some of the most vivid food memories of my childhood revolve around the ice-cream van turning up in our road on summer afternoons with its distinctive tune and dieselly smell. But I would have happily traded the ice-cream van for a real-life muffin man.

I am quite sure that many children today do not realise that the muffin man is not a fictional character in a foodie nursery rhyme, like Jack Horner or Little Miss Muffet, but a very real phenomenon on the streets of England until as recently as the 1930s. He would carry on his head a tray of freshly baked muffins covered with green baize and a white cloth, announce his trade with a loud hand-bell, and sell to private houses and gentlemen's clubs in time for the muffins to be split, toasted on an open fire, slathered with butter and enjoyed for tea.

Milly-Molly-Mandy is lucky enough to buy muffins for a special tea from an itinerant seller in 'Milly-Molly-Mandy Has Friends'. She is doubly fortunate in that Muvver is the kind of home-maker who has a 'baking day' on Saturdays and who invites Milly-Molly-Mandy's friends over for muffins and cherry cake. Everyone's cup runneth over in this delightful little scene:

"They sat in a row before the blazing fire and toasted muffins on forks… and as they toasted the muffins Grandma buttered them and stood them in the muffin dish on the stove to keep warm… And what with the hot muffins, and the cherry cake, and the big dish of strawberry jam, and the honey, and the new brown loaf and the white loaf, the kitchen began to smell very nice indeed… And then everybody talked and laughed and ate and the fire blazed and crackled. And every

single one of the toasted muffins was eaten up."

These days, when we say 'muffin' we must distinguish between the American muffin which requires baking powder as a raising agent, is baked in the oven, and is generally spongy and often sweet, and the traditional English, muffin man, yeast-leavened, unsweetened version which is cooked on a griddle.

I cannot stress enough the superiority of a home-made muffin over a shop-bought muffin. Gather friends and family, and prepare to be converted to the real thing.

MAKES 12–15 MUFFINS
350—375 g strong white flour
100 g plain flour
10 g sea salt
250 ml lukewarm water
150 ml lukewarm milk
15 g fresh yeast or 1 dessertspoon dried yeast
1 teaspoon sugar or runny honey
1 dessertspoon mild olive oil, plus extra for greasing
Rice flour or semolina, for dusting

2 baking trays, oiled, and 1 griddle or wide, flat heavy frying pan

1. It is important to warm the flour before starting. Do this by putting 350 g of the strong white flour, the plain flour and the salt into a large bowl that has been warmed with hot water then dried. Alternatively, place the bowl and ingredients in a low oven (150°C/Gas Mark 2) for 5 minutes or microwave on high for 15–20 seconds.

2. While the flour is warming, measure the water and milk in a jug and warm slightly to blood heat in a pan or microwave.

3. Place the yeast and sugar or honey in a small bowl, add the liquid and stir well.

4. Make a well in the flour, and pour in the yeast liquid and the oil. With your hand mix to a soft, sticky dough. This is not an easy dough to knead by hand and it may be easier to leave it in the bowl and knead by pushing and turn- ing against the sides of the bowl, or to use an electric mixer. Alternatively, turn it out on to a floured surface and knead for 5–7 minutes until it is elastic and smooth and no longer sticky. If the dough is too sticky to handle, add a little more flour as and when you need it. You will find, though, that once

you start kneading, the dough comes together quite easily.

5. Lightly grease the bowl with oil and shape the dough into a ball. Place the dough in the bowl, cover with clingfilm or a damp tea towel and leave in a warm place to rise for 60–90 minutes or until the dough has doubled in size.

6. Punch the dough down and knead gently for 30 seconds. With floured hands, divide the dough into 12–15 equal pieces. Sprinkle each piece with rice flour or semolina and shape into flattened balls. Place these well apart on the baking tray and sprinkle again with rice flour or semolina. You don't want the muffins to rise up too much during the second proving, so it's best to cover them with a layer of clingfilm and a lightweight baking tray while they rise in a warm place for 30–45 minutes.

7. When you are ready to cook the muffins, heat the griddle or frying pan over a gentle heat. With a palette knife or fish slice transfer a few muffins to the hot griddle with the side that was uppermost during the second rising now face down on the surface. Cook slowly over a moderate heat (no hotter) for 6–8 minutes on each side until the surfaces are nicely golden brown. They are cooked when the sides spring back when pressed. Remove from the griddle and put in a warm muffin dish or wrap in a clean tea towel while you cook further batches.

8. Muffins are best eaten immediately or on the day they are cooked. Purists argue that they should not be split and toasted but should be opened slightly at the joint all the way round, toasted on both sides, torn open and spread thickly with butter. The purists are right.

To make a full Milly-Molly-Mandy-style tea, see Awfully Good New-Made Bread (page 27); Very Nice Last Mouthful Cherry Cake (page 64) and Uncle Ambrose's Strawberry Jam (page 126).

Mrs Beaver's Gloriously Sticky Marmalade Roll

Tea with Mr and Mrs Beaver in *The Lion, the Witch and the Wardrobe*. What a warm and cosy contrast to the permanent winter outside in Narnia, and the threat of the evil, icy Queen. We know the Beavers can be trusted as guides to lead the Pevensie children to Aslan because they are kind, welcoming and hospitable, and they eat good, tasty family food in their snug home, which is full of large hams and strings of onions.

The Beavers cook the children the perfect tea to guard against the cold. There is fresh trout caught just half an hour ago, creamy milk, and as much deep yellow butter as you want with your potatoes. Then there is a sweet treat made by Mrs Beaver herself, a wholesome pudding guaranteed to please good-natured children, "a great and gloriously sticky marmalade roll, steaming hot".

All the time the children are eating this simple, well-cooked food, Edmund is still thinking about Turkish delight and, as the narrator points out, "there's nothing that spoils the taste of good ordinary food half so much as the memory of bad magic food".

The plain food on the Beavers' tea table is a metaphor for honesty and good intentions, while a taste for sophisticated Turkish delight is rooted in dishonesty and bad intentions. We pity Edmund as he slips away from the warmth of the Beavers' home to seek the Queen and more Turkish delight. Marmalade roll may not be luxurious and expensive, but it is morally far superior.

Marmalade roll is another name for marmalade roly-poly and uses exactly the same recipe as jam roly-poly but with a marmalade filling. It's an old-fashioned, sweet and filling pudding, perfect for cold winter teas and will fortify you for an adventure in the snow. Traditionally, a roly-poly pudding is steamed for a couple of hours in a pudding cloth or an old shirt sleeve, from which it emerges pale and puffy and damp. But this version is baked; this method takes far less time and has the advantage of producing a roll that is crisp and golden on the outside and jammily, stickily oozy on the inside. And if it's authenticity you're after, then I assure you that steam will escape as soon as the roll is sliced.

SERVES 4–6

250 g self-raising flour
Pinch of salt
125 g shredded suet (beef or vegetarian)
50 g light brown sugar
5 tablespoons (approx.) best marmalade
Milk, for brushing
Demerara sugar, for sprinkling (optional)
Hot custard or cold cream, to serve

Baking tray, lightly greased with suet

1. Preheat the oven to 200°C/Gas Mark 6.
2. Put the flour into a bowl and stir in the salt, suet and light brown sugar.
3. Gradually add enough water (approx. 100 ml) to make a stiff but not sticky dough.
4. Form the dough into a smooth ball then, on a floured surface, roll it out into a long rectangle about 1 cm thick, 15 cm wide and 30 cm long.

5. Spread a thick layer of marmalade on the surface, leaving a margin of about 1 cm round the edge. Brush a little water around the edges to form a seal.

6. Now roll the dough up (wide edge to wide edge) and pinch the ends together so that the filling doesn't escape during cooking.

7. Place seam-side down on the baking tray, brush with milk, and sprinkle with demerara sugar if desired.

8. Bake for 30–40 minutes until browned.

9. Slice thickly and serve immediately with hot custard or cold cream.

VERY NICE LAST MOUTHFUL CHERRY CAKE

As well as being quite delicious, cherry cake is also a marvellously apt metaphor for food in children's literature. The pale square slices of sponge are like the pages of a book, and the cherries scattered throughout the cake suggest the food moments and descriptions of meals contained in the book. Of course, I want plenty of these, but I prefer to have them nicely spread out and not, as can sometimes happen with both cherry cakes and books, in one large clump.

When I devour a book I like a good ending, and, in the same way, when I eat a cake I want to have a nice last mouthful. So I am delighted that Dick, my very favourite juvenile gourmet and food commentator, thinks along the same lines, except that he enjoys a cake in which all the cherries have sunk to the bottom so that he is absolutely guaranteed a fine last mouthful.

Cherry cake is eaten in many books, but it is particularly popular with adventurous outdoor types and crime-busters. So it's no surprise that it appears in a number of Enid Blyton's books. In *Five Go to Mystery Moor* the children enjoy Mrs Johnson's cherry cake as part of a perfectly planned picnic lunch. They ride to a lovely spot on the heathery moor where larks swoop and sing, and unpack all sorts of sandwiches and "great slices of cherry cake" (quite rightly – there's no point in a thin slice of cherry cake) plus juicy pears and, needless to say, plenty of ginger beer.

"'I like this sort of cherry cake,' said Dick, looking at his enormous slice. 'The cherries have all gone to the bottom. They make a very nice last mouthful!'"

Wonderful.

MAKES 1 LARGE CAKE (SERVES 6–8)

225 g self-raising flour

100 g ground almonds

Finely grated zest of 1 lemon (unwaxed)

275 g glacé cherries (preferably undyed)

225 g butter, softened

225 g caster sugar

3 large eggs

A few drops of almond essence (optional)

2 tablespoons milk

Medium (23 x 13 x 7cm) loaf tin, greased with butter

1. Preheat the oven to 180°C/Gas Mark 4.
2. Sift the flour into a bowl and stir in the ground almonds and the lemon zest.
3. Rinse the cherries in lukewarm water to remove excess syrup, pat them dry with kitchen paper and halve them. Add to the flour and almonds and toss gently to distribute.
4. In a large mixing bowl, cream the butter and sugar until light and fluffy. Beat in the eggs one by one, and the almond essence if using.
5. Tip in the flour, ground almonds and cherries together with the milk, and fold into the mixture, making sure the cherries are well dispersed. Spoon into the loaf tin and bake for 55–60 minutes until a metal skewer inserted in the centre of the cake comes out clean. Check after 45 minutes, and if the top is browning quickly place a double thickness of foil on top of the cake.
6. Leave the cake in its tin on a wire rack to cool, then turn out. Serve in thick slices with ginger beer and a good children's book.

AUNT FANNY'S TREACLY, STICKY GINGER CAKE

In the Famous Five stories, Aunt Fanny and Uncle Quentin play the roles of good cop/bad cop to perfection. Uncle Quentin is usually the short-tempered, unjust and awfully fierce workaholic who shuts himself away in his study and has no time for children or dogs. Aunt Fanny, on the other hand, welcomes George's cousins to Kirrin Cottage and provides a warm reception and good food. She is also happily oblivious of the true details of how they spend their days, and prefers instead to concentrate on manners, clean hands and quietness.

These twin roles are clearly defined in the very first book, *Five on a Treasure Island*. After a rather thrilling day on Kirrin Island during which the sea throws up a shipwreck in a spectacular storm, Aunt Fanny is ready and waiting to give Julian, Dick, Anne and George tea at Kirrin Cottage:

"It wasn't long before all four were sitting down to a good tea. Aunt Fanny had baked new scones for them, and had made a ginger cake with black treacle. It was dark brown and sticky to eat. The children finished it all up and said it was the nicest thing they had ever tasted."

Rather than get to the bottom of their obvious excitement, Aunt Fanny is more concerned about the kicking going on under the table (to prevent Anne from spilling the beans about the day's events) and making sure they all wash their sticky hands:

"'... yes, George, I know they're sticky, because *I* made that gingerbread, and you've had three slices! Then you had better go and play quietly... but don't disturb your father, George.'"

And Uncle Quentin doesn't emerge from his study even for a slice of this

delicious ginger cake. Surely his top-secret scientific work can't be *that* interesting?

The recipe that follows makes the most successfully sticky, treacly ginger cake I have ever tasted.

MAKES 1 LARGE LOAF

225 g plain flour	*285 ml milk*
1 teaspoon mixed spice	*1 egg*
3 teaspoons ground ginger	*85 g butter*
1 ½ level teaspoons baking powder	*85 g black treacle*
½ teaspoon bicarbonate of soda	*85 g golden syrup*
½ level teaspoon salt	*115 g caster sugar*

900-g loaf tin, lightly greased with butter and lined with baking parchment

1. Preheat the oven to 180°C/Gas Mark 4.
2. Sift the flour, spices, baking powder, bicarbonate of soda and salt into a large mixing bowl.
3. Measure out the milk in a jug and beat in the egg.
4. Put the butter, treacle, golden syrup and sugar in a pan and heat gently, stirring occasionally, until the butter has melted.
5. Pour this treacle mix on to the ingredients, followed by the milk and egg mix, and beat with a wooden spoon until the contents of the bowl are well mixed.
6. Pour the mixture into the loaf tin and bake for 1½ hours or until the gingerbread is well risen and feels firm to the touch.
7. Leave the cake in its tin until it is cool enough to handle, then turn it out on to a wire rack to cool completely.
8. Conventional wisdom has it that it should now be wrapped up in greaseproof paper and foil and stored for a few days before eating, as this makes the gingerbread more sticky and gingery. However, Famous Five wisdom holds that Aunt Fanny's Ginger Cake is amazing when eaten fresh and still warm.

Great Fruit Cake

It comes in slabs, slices, hunks and chunks. It is found in knapsacks, bicycle baskets, wicker baskets, hampers, tuck boxes. It is served at match teas, nursery teas, afternoon teas and high teas. It is dense, moist and perfectly portable. It goes with cocoa, lemonade, ginger beer, jam tarts, ripe plums, golden apples, and potted meat sandwiches. It is, of course, good, old-fashioned, reliable fruit cake and it pops up everywhere in children's fiction.

There's something quite hearty and reassuring about a fruit cake; it's the workhorse of the tea table or picnic, the solid, filling cake that never lets you down. And even though there is such a thing as a mean, dry, impoverished fruit cake, I am quite sure that all the ones in children's literature are meant to be generously fruity and and rich.

Fruit cake is the kind of cake a mother or nanny or cook would bake to ensure that the children in their care are not going to run out of energy. So in *Upper Fourth at Malory Towers*, when Gwen and Clarissa go to tea with Clarissa's old nurse, Mrs Lucy caters accordingly (she also mistakenly thinks the whole class is coming – hence the enormous spread).

"Set on a table inside was a most marvellous home-made tea! There were tongue sandwiches with lettuce, hard-boiled eggs to eat with bread-and-butter, great chunks of new-made cream cheese, potted meat, ripe tomatoes... gingerbread cake fresh from the oven, shortbread, a great fruit cake with almonds crowding the top, biscuits of all kinds and six jam sandwiches."

With the almonds on top, the fruit cake sounds like Dundee cake, and it so happens that the fruit cake I bake most frequently is one that uses the Dundee cake recipe I discovered years ago. I have adapted it over time, and it makes absolutely the best fruit cake I have ever tasted. It's not as dark and dense and treacly as Christmas cake, and it's not as pale and crumbly as traditional Dundee cake. Instead it's deep golden brown, sweet and juicy. It can be called a Dundee cake if you add the traditional pattern of whole almonds on the top, but I don't bother with this.

It's our standard family fruit cake which I bake to take when we have a holiday in Britain. It's just perfect enjoyed in the afternoon with tea or lemonade, while sitting outside on a stripy deckchair surrounded by books and newspapers and, we hope, blue skies.

MAKES 1 LARGE CAKE

170 g plain flour

120 g self-raising flour

½ teaspoon mixed spice

¼ nutmeg, grated

60 g ground almonds

150 g glacé cherries

350 g sultanas

250 g raisins

Grated zest of 1 lemon (unwaxed)

250 g butter, softened

250 g light soft brown sugar

4 eggs

18 blanched whole almonds (optional)

20-cm round cake tin, greased with butter, lined with baking parchment and wrapped in newspaper (see Step 1)

1. Preheat the oven to 140°C/Gas Mark 2. Wrap a good layer of newspaper round the outside of the cake tin to prevent the cake burning while cooking; take four sheets of newspaper and cut long strips that are just a little taller than the depth of the cake tin. Wrap round the outside and tie tightly with string.

2. First, prepare the dry ingredients. Sift the flours and spices into a bowl and stir in the ground almonds.

3. Next, prepare the fruits. Rinse the glacé cherries in warm water, pat or shake them dry, slice them in half and put them in a second bowl with the sultanas,

raisins and lemon zest.

4. In a large mixing bowl, cream the butter and the sugar until pale and fluffy. Beat in the eggs one at a time.

5. Tip in the flour, spices and fruit and fold in gently with a large metal spoon, making sure all the ingredients are incorporated.

6. Spoon into the cake tin. Wet one hand with cold water and use the back of your hand to smooth the surface. Arrange the whole almonds on top, if using.

7. Bake for approximately 2¼–2¾ hours or until a skewer or sharp knife inserted in the cake comes out clean. Leave the cake in its tin on a wire rack to cool before turning it out and wrapping it in foil.

This cake keeps well for up to a fortnight if wrapped in foil and stored in a tin.

Diana's Favourite Fruity Fruit Cake

Is there anything in life more unjust than unevenly distributed fruit in a fruit cake? The answer is: not when you are young and someone else is slicing the cake. The terrible conviction that you will be the recipient of the least fruity slice while everyone else's piece is clearly packed with dark, gleaming raisins, juicy golden sultanas and glossy glacé cherries, is one of childhood's greatest trials.

It is the kind of worry that adults never seem to understand, but Miss Pepper in Enid Blyton's *The Rockingdown Mystery* is an exception. Despite her name and thin, prim appearance, Miss Pepper harbours a secret knowledge and understanding of children's appetites, so when it comes to afternoon tea in the oak-panelled dining room of Rockingdown Cottage, baked by the local cook Mrs Round (whose very name suggests a generous hand with the fruit), Miss Pepper quietly indulges Diana's delight as they work their way through "a very good tea, with home-made jam, home-produced honey, scones, and a big fruit cake".

"'This is the kind of fruit cake I like,' said Diana, taking a third slice. 'You don't have to look and see if you've got any fruit in your slice – there's plenty all over the cake.'

'You're a pig, Di,' said Roger.

'People are always pigs at your age,' said Miss Pepper."

Diana's favourite fruity fruit cake is light enough for three slices to be enjoyed in addition to jam, honey and scones, yet sufficiently fruity for Diana to feel confident that every slice will meet her high standards. You can be sure it will fill the Dianas and Rogers of this world with enough energy to go exploring, bird-watching and staying up all night to spy on a gang of villains.

MAKES 1 MEDIUM CAKE (SERVES 6–8)

275 g sultanas	*1 heaped teaspoon baking powder*
175 g raisins	*¼ teaspoon ground mixed spice*
50 g mixed peel	*¼ nutmeg, grated*
120 g undyed glacé cherries, halved	*175 g butter, at room temperature*
Grated zest of 1 lemon (unwaxed)	*125 g soft brown sugar*
Juice of 1 orange	*1 dessertspoon runny honey*
225 g plain flour	*3 eggs*

18-cm round cake tin, greased with butter and lined with baking parchment

1. Preheat the oven to 140°C/Gas Mark 2.
2. Place all the fruit in a bowl, add the lemon zest and orange juice and stir well. Leave to one side until needed. (This can be done several hours in advance if preferred.)
3. Sift the flour, baking powder, mixed spice and nutmeg into a bowl.
4. In a separate large bowl, cream the butter and sugar until pale and fluffy. Beat in the honey. Beat the eggs in one at a time, making sure each one is incorporated into the mix. Sift the dry ingredients into the bowl, tip in the fruit mix, and fold in gently with a large metal spoon.
5. Spoon the mixture into the cake tin and lightly smooth the surface. Bake for 1½– 2 hours, checking after an hour to make sure that the cake is not browning too quickly. If it is, place a sheet of foil on top of it.
6. At the end of cooking, test for doneness by inserting a metal skewer or sharp knife in the cake. When the skewer or knife comes out clean, the cake is cooked.
7. Leave the cake in its tin to cool on a wire rack for 10–15 minutes, then turn it out. When it is completely cool, wrap it in foil if you're not serving it immediately. A fruity fruit cake is actually better after a day or two, and will keep for up to a week in an airtight container.

Mrs Glump's
Melt-in-the-Mouth
Shortbread

Snubby is one of Enid Blyton's greatest creations and, as such, he deserves much wider recognition. In the "Barney Mysteries" he's the lovable clown with a particular fondness for cooks and sausages. He's cheeky, disorganised, exuberant and very funny. He is both a gourmand and a gourmet and, with his appreciation of the finer points of baking, a cook's ideal recipient. During term-time he thinks of nothing but home-cooked food; he squeezes and hugs cooks when they bake for him, and his biggest worry is that one day he'll have to grow up and exercise self-control.

"'You know I always feel frightfully sorry for you grown-ups, Miss Pepper. It must be awful never to have a really good tuck-in because you feel it might be rude or greedy.'"

So if Snubby approves of a batch of shortbread, you can be sure it's of the highest quality. In *The Rubadub Mystery* Snubby, Diana, Roger and Miss Pepper are on the beach having tea provided by the gloriously named Mrs Gloria Glump who runs the inn where they are staying. It comprises "a quite enormous number of sandwiches, slices of fruit cake and some home-made shortbread biscuits that really melted in their mouths.

'This is some tea!' said Snubby, with much appreciation."

Shortbread really should melt in your mouth, and for this to happen you need good-quality butter and a very light touch. It should be made quickly and handled as little as possible. I've tried many different recipes in my search for melt-in-the-mouth shortbread and this is undoubtedly the best.

MAKES 18–20 SHORTBREAD BISCUITS (depending on size of cutter)
170 g butter, softened
85 g caster sugar, plus extra for sprinkling
230 g plain flour
30 g cornflour

2 baking trays, lined with baking parchment; 1 round biscuit cutter, approx. 7.5 cm

1. Preheat the oven to 180°C/Gas Mark 4.
2. In a large mixing bowl, beat the butter until creamy with a wooden spoon or electric mixer. Add the sugar and beat until pale and fluffy.
3. Sift the flour and cornflour on to the mix and work them in with a wooden spoon or your hand until the dough comes together.
4. Place the dough on a floured surface and knead gently a few times to make it smooth and rollable.
5. With a wooden rolling pin, roll the dough out to a thickness of about 5 mm then cut out rounds with the biscuit cutter.
6. Place the rounds slightly apart on the baking trays. Knead the trimmings into a ball, roll it out and cut out more rounds. Repeat until all the dough is used up. Prick each round with a fork a few times and sprinkle with caster sugar.
7. Bake for 12–15 minutes or until the shortbread is firm but still pale (do not leave it to turn golden or, worse still, brown).
8. Transfer the trays to a wire rack and leave the biscuits to cool completely. Short-bread is at its most melting when freshly baked but fully cooled.

Tom's Ghostbusting Tea

It is perhaps not surprising that many stories of ghosts, fairies and insubstantial beings do not contain much in the way of food. The books are as calorie-free, light and ethereal as the characters themselves who require nothing in the way of sustenance in order to haunt, fly and move through walls.

But should a ghost story happen to contain a real child, the author can use food in order to make clear the difference between a character who is earthbound by bodily needs, and an insubstantial character who can appear and disappear at will. So we know from his appreciation of his Aunt Gwen's Devonshire tea and his regular midnight forays to the fridge that Tom of Tom's Midnight Garden *is very much a living, hungry child.*

Up until the moment when Tom discovers what happens in the garden at midnight, the only recompense for being sent away from home in order to avoid measles is the food his well-meaning aunt offers him. His first tea in exile is the highlight of an otherwise miserable day, and it's a fine, caring, cheering tea of "boiled eggs, home-made scones and home-made strawberry jam and whipped cream". It's clear that he won't die of malnutrition in his aunt and uncle's staid and quiet flat, although he might just die of boredom.

That is, until the ghostly adventures begin on the stroke of the thirteenth hour…

PROPER SUPPERS

When I say supper, I don't mean it in the sense of the new usage of the word, which has come to indicate an informal or family evening meal. I'm afraid I'm too much of an unreconstructed, old-fashioned supper-lover to be able even to utter the word in any context other than that of a late-evening or late-night snack or treat accompanied by a drink. Although I could perhaps be tempted to expand my interpretation this by the spectacular supper that Maria in *The Little White Horse* enjoys when she arrives at Moonacre:

"The supper was delicious. There was home-made crusty bread, hot onion soup, delicious rabbit stew, baked apples in a silver dish, butter the colour of marigolds, a big blue jug of mulled claret, and hot roasted chestnuts folded in a napkin."

Supper should be easy to make, warming and comforting, but never dull. It should consist of something light and tasty that won't stop anyone settling down for the night. It can include a savoury recipe when it replaces a larger tea or dinner, or when it's eaten after a super-active day, but it's important that it is soothing and relaxing (it's not surprising that hot, milky drinks feature so frequently at bedtime).

Supper is also a time to improvise, and children often have a wonderfully imaginative approach to this meal. Like all good, proper suppers, some of the best fictional ones are made with a mish-mash of leftovers, serendipitous discoveries of what's in the larder or food cupboard, and a dash of spontaneity.

As well as the recipes in this chapter, see Mr Tumnus' Toasty Tea (page 52); Paddington's Favourite Marmalade Buns (page 37); Camp-Fire Cocoa (page 165).

Milly-Molly-Mandy, Little-Friend-Susan and Billy Blunt's Fried Onions

'*Fâites simple*,' said Escoffier, the legendary chef and writer. It's a great piece of advice when it comes to cooking, and one which Milly-Molly-Mandy and her friends heed instinctively when they make supper on their own one evening.

In a story which is unthinkable nowadays, Milly-Molly-Mandy and little-friend-Susan are left on their own with instructions to look after themselves. As soon as the adults have left, they don their aprons and set about the housekeeping in a very grown-up way. When Billy Blunt arrives they decide to fry some onions as a treat. Although Milly-Molly-Mandy isn't allowed to use a bread knife, it's all all right because Billy is a boy and can use his handy penknife to slice the onion. They proceed to fill the kitchen with the delicious smell of frying onions, and everyone's mouth waters, including the reader's.

In fact, it smells so good that when the adults return, they make their own fried onions even though the idea would never have occurred to them if it wasn't for Milly-Molly-Mandy. It's a lovely reminder of how children can see excitement and delight in something quite ordinary, and how Milly-Molly-Mandy's enthusiasm for simple fried onions makes the adults review the value and joy of a simple dish.

Milly-Molly-Mandy is right; fried onions are a treat and they are at their finest when improvised and spontaneous. The keys to great fried onions are fine slicing, medium (not high) heat and long cooking, as Milly-Molly-Mandy, whose onions end up either black or not cooked at all, discovers. Allow at least one medium to

large onion per person (they cook down to very little). Milly-Molly-Mandy et al. fry their onions in beef dripping, the traditional fat for onions, chips and roast potatoes. It does give brilliant results, but you may prefer to fry your onions in something a little more contemporary.

Onions
Beef dripping or mild olive oil and butter
Salt
Pepper

1. Slice the onions thinly so that you will end up with lovely, long, glossily slithery strands.
2. Warm a large frying pan and add a good lump of dripping, or a slosh of oil with

a knob of butter. Let the butter foam and mix with oil.

3. Slide in the sliced onions and stir thoroughly with a wooden spatula to make sure all the onions are covered with the dripping or oil. You can add dripping, or more oil or butter, if you think there isn't enough – or when it looks like the onions are beginning to stick. You don't want the onions to burn, just to caramelise gently.

4. Leave to cook for 20 minutes, stirring occasionally, or until the onions have turned soft and are reddish brown. Season lightly with salt and pepper and serve.

Fried onions are excellent with many fast supper foods such as beefburgers, hot dogs, sausages and mash, warm salads, or just soft bread and butter. Or, even simpler, do as Milly-Molly-Mandy and friends do, throw all caution and any cares about cholesterol to the wind, and eat your fried onions with fried bread.

MUVVER'S LID POTATOES

A special glow surrounds the Milly-Molly-Mandy stories written by the splendidly named Joyce Lankester Brisley. I can still remember basking in its warmth as a child, and I loved rediscovering its simple, cosy, sweet-natured charm when I read the tales to my own children. It is so pervasive and seductive that I am quite sure thousands and thousands of young readers have used their fingers to trace the map of the village where Milly-Molly-Mandy lives, surreptitiously coloured it in to give it Technicolor reality, and wished themselves into it. And one of the finest, warmest examples of the Milly-Molly-Mandy glow is the story in which little-friend-Susan comes for what we would call a sleepover but which Miss Lankester Brisley terms a 'visit'.

I find it endearing that these two little girls view what to us is a commonplace occurrence, a friend to stay the night, as a very special event, and revel in every detail. As a result, the idea of sitting on stools in front of the fire, wearing your red dressing gown (Milly-Molly-Mandy) and Grandma's red shawl (little-friend-Susan)

and having supper with the dog and cat at your side, is quite wonderful, and suddenly much better than any amount of popcorn in front of a screen. There are no sweets, crisps, fizzy drinks or DVDs, but there *are* Muvver's lid potatoes, and I know which I'd prefer.

SERVES 2 LITTLE GIRLS

"First Muvver took two well-baked potatoes out of the oven. Then she nearly cut the tops off them – but not quite. Then she scooped all the potato out of the skins and mashed it up with a little salt and a little pepper and a lot of butter. And then she pushed it back into the two potato-skins, and shut the tops like little lids."

Muvver's lid potatoes are best served with a mug of milk and a plate of bread and butter, and are most delicious when eaten with a little spoon in front of the fire, so that you glow both inside *and* out.

HEIDI'S GRANDFATHER'S SIMPLE SWISS CHEESE AND BREAD SUPPER

If there was one book that made me want to renounce all my worldly goods (trolls, Sindy dolls, Fuzzy Felt, Monopoly board) and move to the mountains to live a plain and good life, that book was *Heidi* by Johanna Spyri. When I first read it, I was entranced by the possibility of supreme simplicity in the Swiss Alps; there is something powerfully seductive about the idea of living in a hut, sleeping on a bed of hay in a loft, spending your days in the company of Peter and the goats, and picking pretty primulas to put in your apron pocket.

Not to mention the Swiss bread and cheese. I would even have traded my weekly packet of Opal Fruits, bought with my 'spends', for a taste of the plain but intensely evocative meals that Heidi enjoys with her grandfather. Although she is thrilled with the luxury of white bread rolls in Frankfurt, it is the dark, long-lasting bread, enjoyed with cheese and fresh, steaming goats' milk, that comes to symbolise all she misses when she is taken away from her beloved mountains.

Heidi and her initially none-too-welcoming grandfather bond over their first supper together; Heidi watches him prepare the toasted cheese to go with the round bread: "As the pot began to sing, he put a large piece of cheese on a toasting fork and moved it to and fro in front of the fire until it became golden yellow all over."

Their suspicions about each other begin to fade as they share this significant meal, and the unwanted five-year-old Heidi begins to charm her grumpy grandfather with her sweet and sincere nature. It's as if his resistance melts with the cheese…

Sourdough bread or rye bread   *Gruyere cheese, cut into 3-cm cubes*
Fresh milk (goats' milk optional)   *Long-handled fork or toasting fork*

1. Imagine you are in a wooden hut on the side of a snowy mountain. You can see the stars shining brightly in the clear night sky. Worries, work, mortgages and bills do not exist for the moment.
2. Stoke the fire until red and glowing.
3. Slice the bread thickly.
4. Pour the fresh milk into mugs.
5. Place a piece of cheese on the fork and swivel and turn it until it bubbles all over and turns a darker, golden colour.
6. Transfer quickly to a slice of bread.
7. Eat while hot. Repeat as necessary.

THE BORROWERS' POTTED SHRIMPS

I magine a quirky, improvised doll's house under the floorboards, the kind a child might put together with all the things that can be found lying around a house. It has beds made out of cigar boxes, a wristwatch for a wall clock, postage stamps for portraits and cotton reels for stools. But best of all, it is inhabited by real, four-inch-high people who come out when it's quiet to 'borrow' more things and, most importantly, food.

This is the sublimely imagined and described world of *The Borrowers* in which tiny, doll-like portions of food are served, and in which a single potted shrimp is a wonderful treat. After Arrietty's first borrowing expedition (and meeting with a 'Human Bean') she and Pod come back to their home. As well as roast sliced chest-nuts to eat with butter like toast and tea from a hollow oak-apple, there is "a plate of hot dried currants, well plumped before the fire; there were cinnamon crumbs, crispy golden, and lightly dredged with sugar, and in front of each place, oh, delight of delights, a single potted shrimp" served on silver plates – florins for Arrietty and Homily and a half-crown for Pod.

If only everyone could appreciate the delight of potted shrimps, singular or plural. They are one of England's greatest traditional tea-time treats yet they are in danger of disappearing from its culinary map. The small brown shrimp is relatively expensive, difficult to obtain and fiddly to peel, but when 'potted' it soaks up butter and fragrant spices beautifully.

You can sometimes find small packs of Morecambe Bay potted shrimps in supermarkets, or you can have a lovely time making your own. You may have to

85

pre-order your brown shrimps from a fishmonger, or you can replace them with small, pink shrimps. But if you do use the far superior brown shrimp, it's best to adopt a Borrower approach and see each one as a single, delicious treat.

In keeping with this approach, I have borrowed this recipe from Mrs Beeton. Potted shrimps taste best when their flavour has developed during a day or two in the fridge.

SERVES 4
80 g butter, plus melted butter to cover
2 blades of mace
Pinch of cayenne pepper (optional)
Freshly grated nutmeg
400 g peeled brown shrimps
Hot toast, butter and lemon wedges, to serve

4 small ramekins

1. Put the butter, mace, cayenne if using, and a little grated nutmeg into a medium pan and allow the butter to melt gently over a low heat.
2. Pat the shrimps with kitchen paper to remove excess moisture, then add them to the pan. Stir gently, allow them to heat through and leave on a low heat for 5 minutes; do not let the liquid boil.
3. Remove the mace blades, divide the shrimps and butter between the four ramekins and level the tops.
4. Leave in the fridge to cool, then spoon a thin layer of melted butter over the shrimps and allow it to set.
5. Serve the shrimps with hot toast (brown for preference), more butter and lemon wedges. (I, for one, do not borrow Pod's idea of eating potted shrimps with a slice of boiled chestnut.)

The Edwardian Larder

I'm taking liberties here with the definition of 'Edwardian' because even though some her best-known stories were written at the tail end of Queen Victoria's reign, E. Nesbit is generally regarded as a quintessentially Edwardian children's writer. And her books contain a quintessentially Edwardian larder.

Food is of utmost importance to E. Nesbit's characters and her oeuvre remains to this day the most wonderful repository of everything we associate with early twentieth-century food, cooking and treats. The sheer range of eatables, with its strange mix of ultra-English-plain and unfamiliar-Empire-exotic, is astonishing, and the peep into her fictional larder allows hungry readers to discover what children ate a hundred years ago.

The generally accepted view is that they ate boring and bland nursery food while the adults downstairs ate opulent, richly luxurious banquets all the time. But E. Nesbit's children enjoy a tremendously varied diet.

It's a world of suet pudding and buying penny currant buns by the dozen and clapping them together and eating them as a triple-decker sandwich (see illustration opposite), and ginger beer, and sponge cakes out of a glass jar on a bar counter, and hashed mutton, and cold tongue, and rice pudding, and mixed candied peel, and chestnuts, and acid drops, and bread and butter pudding, and minced veal, and biscuits with caraways, and beefsteak and kidney pudding, and red gooseberries, and semolina pudding, and custard puddings, and apple turnovers, and soda-water siphons, and cold-mutton days, and nursery tea, and being denied dinner as punishment for bad behaviour.

It's one in which you can go to the fair and spend ninepence on "some Barcelona nuts, red-streaked apples, small sweet yellow pears, pale pasty

gingerbread, a whole quarter of a pound of peppermint bullseyes, and two bottles of ginger-beer". Or gaze through the windows of bakers' shops at "jam tarts and Swiss rolls and Victoria sandwiches and Bath buns". And there are even a few adults (such as generous uncles) who indulge children and provide treats such as butterscotch, peppermint bullseyes, raspberry noyau, hardbake, peppermint rock and ginger wine.

E. Nesbit is incredibly well attuned to children's appetites and she never lost her childlike sensibility to the verbal joys of food. But she also has a long memory of the joys of childish indulgences; when she was young, she used to climb up to the roof of the family house to escape the adults and to eat and read. Later she wrote of that time, "Happy vanished days, when to be on the roof and to eat tinned pineapple in secret constituted happiness". She knew at first hand the combined pleasures of eating and reading, and she made quite sure that her readers, too, never went hungry.

CREAMY RICE PUDDING

The Edwardian period was the heyday of the pudding and no supper menu was complete without at least one. Children, in particular, ate huge amounts of filling, stodgy puddings to fill them up and keep them warm. These days, though, we don't regard them as treats, and this is where we go wrong. Rice pudding can be a wonderfully satisfying and delicious evening treat when made with quality ingredients and a generous spirit.

The problem is that so many people are put off rice pudding by horrible, watery, tasteless school versions or sticky, glutinous tinned varieties. I think we need to reinstate it, so here's a recipe for one that is a treat, not a penance. It is a rich, creamy, sweet and gentle reincarnation of a great Edwardian pudding made glorious once more.

There are three things to note about rice pudding. The first is that you should make far more than you think you'll need because everyone will be so converted they'll soon be eating it from the dish. Secondly, allow for periodic checks and stirs; rice pudding cannot be left completely for a few hours despite what some recipes say – it does need to be tended to occasionally. Having said that, it's not exactly demanding to make. Finally, the best rice pudding is made with the best milk: full-cream Channel Islands milk is perfect. Allow for 3 hours' cooking time.

SERVES 4–6

25 g butter

100 g short-grain pudding rice

70 g sugar

1 vanilla pod or a few drops vanilla
   extract

1 litre full-cream milk

Nutmeg

Fresh cream, raspberry or strawberry
   jam, and/or golden syrup, to serve

Shallow ovenproof dish

1. Preheat the oven to 140°C/Gas Mark 1.
2. Use half the butter to grease the ovenproof dish.
3. Place the rice, sugar, vanilla and the rest of the butter in the dish. Pour in 500 ml of the milk and stir gently to mix.
4. Place in the oven. After 1 hour, add a further 400 ml of the milk, stir and return the pudding to the oven.
5. After 2 hours, stir again and add a little of the remaining milk if necessary. Grate the nutmeg on top, and return to the oven.
6. After 3 hours, take the pudding out of the oven, remove the vanilla pod, if using, and serve with fresh cold cream, jam and/or golden syrup for full treat effect.

ELLEN'S EXTREMELY COMFORTING POSSET

Posset is the drink that will be for ever associated with *The Box of Delights* by John Masefield. It is one of those ancient British drinks with funny-sounding names such as caudle, purl, metheglin, flip, nog and syllabub. We generally don't make these any more and, should we want to, we discover that there is no definitive recipe, because in the past everyone just knew how to make a warm, spicy, milky, eggy, soothing drink. Just like that.

Just like Ellen, in fact. When Kay is perplexed by events and is struggling to solve the mysteries that beset him, he admits he should do as the Inspector of Police might advise, and laugh and take a posset. So he turns to Ellen and asks her to make him one because he's feeling so miserable. Ellen dutifully whips up a big mug of posset which he drinks in bed:

"He drank it down, thinking that the Inspector certainly knew a good thing. After he had drunk it the comfort seemed to tingle through him, which put an end to his miseries."

And he is out like a light.

The speed with which Kay falls asleep suggests that the 'tingling comfort' must in fact be closely connected to a fair whack of alcohol, such as brandy or sherry. Posset was not only known as a traditional Christmas drink and a drink for invalids, but also as a bedtime drink to help children sleep in the days when it was commonplace to use alcohol to 'soothe' them. But as this is unacceptable nowadays, I have experimented with several old recipes and the one that follows can be made with or without the alcohol. Both versions are extremely comforting.

SERVES 2–4
600 ml full-cream milk
½ lemon (unwaxed)
Nutmeg
2–3 teaspoons soft brown sugar
1–2 tablespoons brandy, rum or sherry (optional)
1 egg

1. Have cups or mugs ready.
2. Gently heat the milk until it is almost at boiling point. Remove from the heat and put the pan on a heatproof surface.
3. Grate the zest of the lemon and a good amount of nutmeg into the milk and whisk well. Now whisk in the sugar, to taste.
4. Add the alcohol, if using, and taste again.
5. Add the egg and immediately whisk it into the liquid – you don't want it to scramble in the heat of the milk.
6. Pour the posset into the cups or mugs, hand out to waiting sleepyheads/merry-makers and inhale the wonderful aromas before sipping and sleeping.

A Funny and Delightful Supper

There's something quite magical about improvised late-night meals; when I was little I loved my Nana's 'surprise suppers' at her house. My brother and I weren't allowed into the kitchen while she was putting one together, but had to wait until she came into the lounge with a tray full of all the little treats she could find in her fridge and larder. There was no cohesion to the selection, and it was more like a culinary jumble sale than a proper meal, but to us it tasted far, far better than anything planned.

The keys to a surprise or "funny and delightful supper", such as the one enjoyed in *The Railway Children* when the mother and three children arrive in the dark at their new house in the country, are ease of eating and unusual combinations. The ingredients must be ready to eat (cold or leftover food is perfect), bite-size (knives and forks should be superfluous) and comprise plenty of small treats (this is a fun meal, after all).

While the children light candles and a fire, Mother concocts a supper with "all the odds and ends out of the store cupboard", which they have brought with them. So she brings in a tray with "biscuits, both the Marie and plain kind, sardines, preserved ginger, cooking raisins, and candied peel and marmalade" and they drink ginger wine and water out of teacups, because they can't find the glasses.

The charm of these suppers is that they are like something campers or explorers would enjoy – in the Antarctic Scott and his men ate strange combinations of high-calorie foods – but within the comfort of your own home (or den). They are economical and easy to make and, who knows, you may even find you like a combination of sardines and marmalade.

EQUIPMENT
- *A large tray*
- *Plenty of small bowls or egg cups to hold the treats*
- *Tablecloth to go on the carpet as picnic cloth (for full camping/exploring effect)*
- *Non-matching teacups and mugs for drinks*

FOOD

The idea is to create a sort of pick 'n' mix of finger food; complementary flavours and textures can be overlooked on this occasion. Suggestions for inclusion:
- *Crisps, nuts, savoury snacks*
- *Popcorn*
- *Small cubes of cheese*
- *Pieces of cold chicken, ham or beef*
- *Grapes, slices of apple/pear/melon/mango, segments of oranges or satsumas*
- *Mini biscuits or jam tarts*
- *Handful of sweets*
- *Squares of chocolate*
- *Small cakes or tiny slices of cake*
- *Dried fruit – raisins, sultanas, cherries, apricots, apples, mangos*
- *Squash, juice, cordial, fizzy drinks, ginger beer*

COOKS' SPECIAL
TREATS

Just as we have legendary cooks in real life, so we also find them in literature. And children's books, unsurprisingly, contain a wealth of wonderful cooks and bakers who are busy whisking and beating and kneading and mixing to make treats for children and, in the process, maintaining the traditions and specialities of hundreds of years.

Some of them, such as Mrs Round and Joanna in Enid Blyton's stories and Debby in the *What Katy Did* novels are a solid, dependable presence in the kitchen, bringing out three meals a day as well as any number of treats for elevenses, afternoon teas and supper. Like the spines of the books themselves, they are the metaphorical backbones that bind characters and stories.

Other cooks have a whiff of sorcery about them, as if they were endowed with magical powers. Bakers such as Marmaduke Scarlet and Digweed in Elizabeth Goudge's books control the goings-on in the kitchen with an air of secrecy and mystery that baffles those around them. They have the ability to read minds, to conjure up exactly what someone wants to eat, and to work at a superhuman pace. Their gruff or strange demeanour contradicts their light touch with syllabubs, sponges, pastries and breads, and no one takes greater pride in their creations than these unlikely chefs.

Then there are the motherly cooks for whom baking is an expression of their care and concern and love for the recipients, no matter how plain or simple the treat. Ma in the Little House stories battles against all odds to cook for her family, Marilla does her best to pass her renowned cooking skills on to the enthusiastic but inattentive Anne of Green Gables, and it is the plain, homely cooking of Dickon's mother, Mrs Sowerby, that brings Colin and Mary back to life in *The Secret Garden*.

Of all the great cooks in books, though, my favourites are the children who have a go at cooking themselves. Milly-Molly-Mandy, Anne of Green Gables, Anne of the Famous Five and Susan in *Swallows and Amazons* are some of the most endearing of all of them. And that's because they want to learn to cook and to make their own treats; and no matter how much you like other cooks' specialities, you never know when it will be your turn to do the baking and to maintain a proud tradition.

As well as the recipes in this chapter, you can find more cooks' specialities throughout the book: Devonshire Splits (page 132) made by Marmaduke Scarlet; Milly-Molly-Mandy, Little-Friend-Susan and Billy Blunt's Fried Onions (page 78), Mate Susan's Scrambled Eggs (page 149), Ma's Pancake Men (page 22) and Marilla's Zero-Alcohol Raspberry Cordial (page 256).

MRS ROUND'S SMASHING TREACLE PUDDING

I've always thought that some foods have deliciously onomatopoeic names. 'Treacle pudding' sounds as sticky, gooey and stolid as it really is, and just uttering the words aloud is guaranteed to make me feel warmer and cosier on a gloomy, grey winter's day.

The itinerant orphan, Snubby, knows the importance of a good treacle pudding. In Enid Blyton's *The Rockingdown Mystery* he is, as ever, concerned about his food:

"'What's for pudding today, Mrs Round? ... Are you going to make us one of your smashing treacle puddings again? Honestly, I wish you'd come and be cook at our school. The boys would cheer you every day.'

Mrs Round beamed and patted the bun of hair at the back of her head. 'Oh, go on with you now!' she said."

But it's a hard cook who can resist such flattery.

With her name and solid presence in the kitchen, Mrs Round is the perfect cook to make a smashing treacle pudding, something to look forward to after a complex adventure involving smugglers; it's what is safe and delicious, not frightening and uncomfortable. It's the essence of care and comfort, and exactly what you need after a long day (or night) restoring the world's moral order.

As Snubby points out, treacle pudding makes the crossover from school to home and vice versa, but it is generally acknowledged that school treacle pudding is a vastly inferior creation to the home-made variety. For a taste of treacle pudding as Mrs Round might make it, it should be damp, hot, filling, darkly sweet and toffee-ish, not soggy, stodgy and tummy-clogging.

Steamed puds are proper puds, ones that in the past would not have caused a full-time cook any inconvenience. They require a little forward planning as they have to steam for several hours and you need to check the water level regularly. But I find the bubbling and rattling a soothing background noise on a Sunday afternoon or evening. I can read the papers or prepare a roast or listen to Radio 4 while the kitchen steams up – it's really not such a trial, believe me. And, call me old-fashioned, but I do believe a treacle pudding should contain treacle.

SERVES 6
3 tablespoons golden syrup
Juice and grated zest of 1 lemon (unwaxed)
170 g soft brown sugar
170 g soft butter
3 eggs
1 tablespoon treacle
170 g self-raising flour
Custard or cream, to serve

Foil and string, plus a large pan and a pudding bowl, greased with butter, that fits inside it comfortably

1. Boil a kettleful of water.
2. Lightly grease the pudding bowl with the butter and put the golden syrup and lemon juice in the bottom of the bowl.
3. In a large mixing bowl, cream the sugar and butter until pale and fluffy. Add the eggs one at a time and mix in well.
4. Add the treacle and lemon zest and sift in the flour. Mix gently with a large metal spoon.

5. Spoon the mix into the pudding bowl.

6. Take a length of foil which, when folded in two, will cover the pudding bowl generously. Make a pleat in the centre and place it over the top of the bowl. Tie securely with string and make a handle with a double piece of string so that the bowl can be lifted easily from the pan (this is really worth doing – if the bowl fits the pan snugly it can be difficult to remove).

7. Carefully lower the bowl into the pan and pour in enough boiling water to come three-quarters of the way up the outside of the bowl.

8. Place on a gentle heat and allow to steam for 2– 2¼ hours. The water should simmer, not boil, and the bowl should rattle gently. Check the water level from time to time to make sure the pan is not drying out and top up as necessary.

9. When the pudding is ready, lift the bowl out of the pan and allow to stand for 5 minutes.

10. Remove the foil and string. Place a large plate on top of the bowl and quickly invert bowl and plate so that the pudding comes out on to the plate (you'll need oven gloves to perform this trick). Let the bowl stand upside down on the plate for 30 seconds so that all the syrupy sauce drains out.

11. Serve with custard or cream.

MARMADUKE SCARLET'S
SAFFRON CAKE

I'm not much of a party girl, but there are a few parties I really wish I'd been invited to – it's just a shame that they are mostly fictional. Tea parties, in particular, are my sort of party and I would love to be a guest at Maria's spectacular one in *The Little White Horse* when Marmaduke Scarlet pulls out all the stops and provides the most wonderful catering imaginable.

As well as being an invitee, I would also enjoy being with him while he prepares the treats for the party. Marmaduke is a strange little cook who possesses almost mystical powers in the kitchen plus the skills and artistry to conjure up all sorts of treats and deliciousness at a moment's notice, and he relishes the planning with the pleasure of a truly dedicated baker:

"… with the fire of inspiration suddenly lighting up his whole face… [he] murmured under his breath, 'Plum cake. Saffron cake. Cherry cake. Iced fairy cakes. Éclair s. Gingerbread. Meringues. Syllabub. Almond fingers. Rock cakes. Chocolate drops. Parkin. Cream horns. Devonshire splits. Cornish pasty. Jam sandwiches. Lemon-curd sandwiches. Lettuce sandwiches. Cinnamon toast. Honey toast…'

'But, surely, Marmaduke, seven people won't eat all that!' interrupted Maria."

(They do, and not a crumb of food is left on the table at the end of the party.)

It would be wonderful to watch this master craftsman at work in his large, sunny, warm, clean kitchen and to learn how to make everything in his mouth-watering list of delicacies. But if I could choose only one, it would be the medieval-sounding saffron cake with its use of the colourful, rare and exotic spice, and its historical connections with the West Country where the book is set. Because no matter how much you roll the words around your tongue, you will never experience the unique, truly distinctive aroma and taste of saffron until you actually smell and taste it.

MAKES 1 LARGE LOAF
½ teaspoon saffron strands
300 ml hot milk
15 g fresh yeast or 1 dessertspoon dried yeast
1 teaspoon sugar
500 g strong white flour
1 teaspoon salt
150 g butter
50 g caster sugar
170 g dried fruit (sultanas, raisins, currants, mixed peel)

900-g loaf tin, greased with butter or oiled

1. Put the saffron in a bowl. Heat the milk, pour it over the saffron and stir. Leave to infuse for at least 30 minutes or, even better, overnight.
2. When you are ready to start the cake, put the yeast and 1 teaspoon sugar in a bowl. Reheat the now saffron-yellow milk until it is lukewarm, but not hot, and pour it over the yeast. Stir to mix and leave while you get on with the remaining ingredients.
3. Sift the flour and salt into a large mixing bowl. Add the butter and rub it into the flour until the mixture resembles fine breadcrumbs. Add the caster sugar and dried fruit and stir into the mix.
4. Make a well in the middle of the flour and pour in the warm milk and yeast mixture. With your hand, work the liquid into the dry ingredients. The dough should be soft but not too sticky. Add a little more milk or flour if necessary to get

103

the consistency right.

5. Turn the dough out on to a floured work surface and knead until it is smooth and elastic. This will take 8–10 minutes.

6. Shape the dough to fit the loaf tin and cover lightly with oiled clingfilm or a damp tea towel. Leave the dough to rise to the top of the tin. This will take 1½–3 hours in a warm room, but the dough can also be left to rise overnight in a cool room.

7. Preheat the oven to 180°C/Gas Mark 4.

8. Bake for 1 hour until the top is golden brown and the base sounds hollow when tapped; you will have to remove the cake from the tin to check this.

9. Leave the cake in its tin on a wire rack to cool completely, then turn it out.

10. Serve fresh (saffron cake does not keep well) with plenty of butter and any, or all, of Marmaduke Scarlet's tea-time treats.

DEBBY'S JUMBLES

Katy "could wait no longer, but crept out of bed, crossed the floor on tiptoe, and raising the lid [of the box] a little put in her hand. Something crumby and sugary met it, and when she drew it out, there, fitting on her finger like a ring, was a round cake with a hole in the middle of it.

'Oh! it's one of Debby's jumbles!' she exclaimed."

When I mentioned on my blog, yarnstorm, that I was writing this book, I had an amazing response from readers who went into raptures about their own favourite books and treats. One treat in particular stood out by dint of it being so well known and yet still a mystery. What exactly are jumbles, the treats that Katy and her sister Clover eat on Christmas morning in *What Katy Did at School*?

Jumbles were popular in England and other European countries during the seventeenth and eighteenth centuries when they were also known as gemmels from the German word for twin, and were so called because they were originally in the shape of two entwined rings. In the nineteenth century they were taken to America where, according to a recipe printed in 1855, they became less hard, more spongy, and circular. A recipe in an American cookery book of 1917 suggests that by then they were softer and thinner and more like sugar cookies, and the central hole had to be cut out with a cutter. Back in England, they eventually turned into flat, crisp, biscuity thins to be served with desserts (as mentioned by Agnes Jekyll who gives a recipe for orange jumbles in *Kitchen Essays*, written in 1922).

But Debby's jumbles are of the ring variety, so that is what this recipe makes. Debby is clearly an accomplished cook (her muffins are light and her clear crab-apple jelly comes out of the mould perfectly) and her jumbles are a wonderful taste

of home for Katy and Clover, who jump excitedly back into bed, to nibble and chat-
ter on Christmas morning.

Jumbles can be flavoured with lemon zest (as in this recipe) or with orange zest,
caraway seeds, almond essence, rosewater or brandy. Just add a few drops of flavouring liquid, half a teaspoon of seeds or grated zest to the basic recipe.

MAKES 12–15 JUMBLES, or enough for a girl to wear rings on her fingers *and* a few
rings on her toes.

120 g butter

150 g caster sugar,
  plus extra for sprinkling

2 eggs

Grated zest of 1 lemon (unwaxed)

270 g self-raising flour

Milk, for brushing

Baking tray, lined with baking parchment

1. Preheat the oven to 180°C/Gas Mark 4.
2. In a mixing bowl, cream the butter and sugar until pale and fluffy.
3. Beat in the eggs one at a time.
4. Add the lemon zest and sift in the flour and gently fold into the mixture with a
   metal spoon.
5. Divide the mixture into 12–15 pieces, roll them out into sausages approximately
   15 cm long and form them into rings. Make sure the holes in the middle are quite
   large as the mixture will spread during baking and you don't want them to close
   up. Place well apart on the baking tray, brush with milk and sprinkle generously
   with caster sugar.
6. Bake for 15–20 minutes until pale golden. Leave the jumbles to cool before wearing and/or eating.

JOANNA OBCBE
GINGER BISCUITS

A lthough there is often no better reward for a cook than seeing the food he has prepared being eaten and enjoyed, he may sometimes deserve a little more recognition. Snubby in Enid Blyton's 'R' Mysteries does his best with squeezes and hugs for cooks, but it is Dick in the Famous Five who articulates what we must all have felt at one time or another, namely that a good cook deserves a medal.

Joanna is the cheerful, plump cook who appears in many of the Famous Five books. She is renowned for her macaroons and mince pies as well as her good temper and kindness. She is a solid, dependable presence in the kitchen and has impeccable timing when it comes to baking. In *Five Go On Kirrin Island Again*, Joanna just happens to have made some of her "delicious ginger biscuits" on the very morning that George has to be parted (albeit temporarily) from her beloved dog Timmy, and these are brought out to cheer her up. It is left to Dick to speak on behalf of the group:

"'I say, aren't these good? You know, I do think good cooks deserve some kind of decoration, just as much as good soldiers or scientists, or writers. I should give Joanna the OBCBE.'"

And, in his role of kitchen diplomat, Dick awards Joanna 'The Order of the Best Cooks of the British Empire'.

These ginger biscuits are quick and easy to make, and are a staple after-school treat in our house. I have never been awarded any sort of decoration for my efforts, but the fact that they disappear within minutes tells me all I need to know.

Makes 20–24 biscuits

120 g soft butter
120 g golden caster sugar
1 dessertspoon golden syrup
1 egg yolk
200 g plain flour
½ teaspoon cream of tartar
½ teaspoon bicarbonate of soda
1 heaped teaspoon ground ginger
Pinch of salt
Pinch of mixed spice (optional)
Pinch of ground cloves and/or ground nutmeg (optional)

Baking tray, lined with baking parchment

1. Preheat the oven to 170°C/Gas Mark 3.
2. In a large mixing bowl, cream the butter and sugar together. Beat in the golden syrup and egg yolk.
3. Sift the flour, cream of tartar, bicarbonate of soda, ginger and salt, and the spices if using, into the bowl and work them in until the mix comes to a firm dough.
4. Break off small pieces of the dough, shape them into balls and place them well apart on the baking tray.
5. Press down lightly with your fingers to partially flatten each biscuit.
6. Bake for 10–12 minutes until the biscuits are golden brown and smelling delicious.
7. Transfer the tray to a wire rack and leave the biscuits to cool.

Pippi's Swedish Pancakes

One of Pippi Longstocking's greatest charms is her 'beginner's mind'. Zen Buddhist philosophers believe that the way to enjoy life to the full is to approach each task as if for the first time, and to bring a freshness and a desire for discovery to each new day. So the untrained, untutored Pippi approaches baking with a completely original and open mind. If a quantity of biscuit dough is too large to fit on a pastry board, why not roll it out on the floor? If an egg needs to be broken, why not fling it up in the air and wait for it to come down into a bowl? If pancake batter needs beating, why not use whichever implement is to hand as long as it does the job, even if it is a bath brush?

Pippi also brings phenomenal energy to her baking and when she makes a pancake for Tommy and Annika it's like a performance out of the circus. An egg lands and breaks on her head, she beats the batter so hard that it spatters on the kitchen walls, she throws the mix on the pan, tosses the cooked pancake up to the ceiling, then hurls it on to a plate. Nevertheless, her ever-admiring audience and recipients eat it and think it "a very good pancake".

Swedish Pancakes are particularly good for beginner bakers to make. The batter can be prepared by adults for children to cook themselves, and older children can undertake the whole process on their own. There is no mystique to pancakes – you just need a good, flat, hot pan and a large spoon to ladle out the mixture. They don't need to be tossed or thrown unless that's your style. And eggs do not need to be caught in bowls in order to be cracked. But it's an impressive trick if you can master it.

MAKES 10–12 PANCAKES

3 eggs
150 g plain flour
½ teaspoon salt
1 tablespoon caster sugar
375 ml milk
Butter, for greasing
Sugar, lemon juice, golden syrup or jam, to serve

Griddle or heavy, flat frying pan.

1. In a large mixing bowl, whisk the eggs, flour, salt and sugar until smooth.
2. Gradually add the milk and beat until the batter is smooth after each addition.
3. Heat the griddle or frying pan and grease it lightly with butter.
4. Spoon a ladleful of the batter on to the griddle or frying pan and quickly tip and swirl the pan to make a thin circle.
5. Cook over a medium heat and when the edge of the pancake is dry and the underside golden, turn it over with a spatula or flip it in the air if you feel like doing tricks. Cook the second side briefly. Serve immediately with whatever accompaniment you prefer.

MA'S HAND-SWEETENED CORNBREAD

"She made the cornmeal and water in two thin loaves, each shaped in a half circle. She laid the loaves with their straight sides together in the bake-oven, and she pressed her hand flat on top of each loaf. Pa always said he did not ask any other sweetening, when Ma put the prints of her hands on the loaves."

What is the cook's equivalent of the gardener's green fingers, I wonder? How is it possible to suggest the magic touch some cooks and bakers have that makes everything they create successful and delicious? Because this is exactly what Laura's Ma is blessed with and it's why I love reading how, in *Little House on the Prairie*, her hands leave both a literal and a metaphorical imprint on cornbread.

Cornbread is the staple food of the Little House family. They eat cornmeal cakes cooked on a camp fire under the vast expanse of sky on their journey to the little house, and they eat cold cornmeal on their journey away from it. In between, they eat it for breakfast and supper, steaming hot, cold, plain or flavoured, and Ma is instructed to bake it when "Red Indians" come visiting.

There is something ineffably reassuring homely, simple and comforting about cornbread. It might be the everyday stuff of many American kitchens, but when you have never encountered or tasted it except when reading Laura Ingalls Wilder's books, it takes on an extra-ordinary dimension. Especially when it is made by Ma with her magic baking hands.

There are so many ways of making cornbread that it's impossible to give a definitive recipe, but this one makes a good-sized, tasty version that is quick and easy to make and, in keeping with Ma's approach, it does not contain any sweetening ingredient such as sugar or honey.

In the United Kingdom it's not that easy to find cornmeal labelled as such, but Italian polenta is exactly the same thing (I use the fine-ground type). Cornflour is *not* suitable.

Cornbread is often flavoured, so you might want to add one or more of the following: crisp pieces of cooked bacon, a chopped fresh green chilli, a couple of sliced spring onions, fried onions.

MAKES 1 LARGE CORNBREAD (SERVES 8)
120 ml milk
90 g butter
240 g cornmeal
240 g plain flour
2 teaspoons baking powder
2 teaspoons bicarbonate of soda
1 teaspoon salt
1 egg
120 ml plain yoghurt or buttermilk

20-cm round tin, greased with butter, the base lined with baking parchment

1. Preheat the oven to 180°C/Gas Mark 4.
2. Warm the milk in a pan. Remove from the heat, add the butter and leave while

the butter melts. Sift the dry ingredients into a large mixing bowl.

3. When the milk and butter liquid is cool, beat in the eggs and yoghurt or butter-milk. Pour into the bowl and mix quickly.

4. Turn the mix into the tin. With a wet hand (otherwise the dough will stick) gently level the surface and press to leave an imprint.

5. Bake for approximately 25 minutes or until the top is golden and the bread is firm to the touch.

6. Turn out and cut into slices or squares. Serve hot and with a sweet smile.

LESSONS IN THE KITCHEN

My first baking memories are of kneeling on a stool in my Nana's kitchen, wearing one of her aprons hitched up to cover my front, while I creamed butter and sugar in a brown bowl with a large wooden spoon. This was my introduction to the warm, sweet pleasures of the kitchen, which helped me to identify with the characters in literature like Milly-Molly-Mandy who bakes with Muvver, Anne of Green Gables who is inspired by Marilla's wonderful cooking and baking skills, and Laura who helps Ma in the pioneer kitchens in the Houses in the Big Woods and on the Prairie. I lapped up all these vicarious kitchen lessons and from an early age was an enthusiastic, if not accomplished, helper and baker.

Baking with an adult is not only the best way to start a baking education, it is also one of the most enjoyable. And it's never too early to start learning, as I found with my children. As soon as they could hold a spoon they were allowed to help stir and whisk and add ingredients. With time they progressed to breaking eggs,

melting chocolate and chopping cherries. Later they began baking independently, each developing their own signature creation (Tom: chocolate cornflake cakes, Alice: éclairs, Phoebe: birthday cakes). Their independence in the kitchen and the pleasure that baking gives them is a fair reward for all the clearing and washing up I undertook to get them started.

Baking is also an excellent way to introduce children to various culinary skills. It is, by and large, an exact science requiring very little guesswork, judgement and tasting (although that never stopped anyone dipping their finger in the bowl) and it's easy to achieve brilliant results by following a recipe to the letter. The end results often belie the simplicity of many recipes, and it's possible to make apparently sophisticated treats such as éclairs and meringues just by adhering to weights, measures, timings, ingredients and instructions. And there is the added incentive of making something you actually want to eat.

The recipes that follow are based on scenes in which children bake with adults. For more recipes suitable for adult and child sessions, see: Ma's Pancake Men (page 22); Red Kitchen Jam Tarts (page 30); Mrs Banks' Bribery and Corruption Cocoanut Cakes (page 54); St Clare's Éclair s (page 205); Mary Poppins' Strike-Me-Pink Raspberry Jam Cakes (page 199); Cook's Immensely Enjoyable Meringues (page 233); Proper-Meeting Rock Buns (page 239); Debby's Jumbles (page 105); Jeremy and Jemima's More-Jam-Than-Puff Jam Puffs (page 185); The Swallows' Squashed Fly Biscuits (page 162).

Milly-Molly-Mandy's Little Patty-Pan Sultana Cakes

There are many reasons why baking with children is so valuable and important, and perhaps one of the most enticing is the discovery of the great pleasures of leftovers. Scraping the bowl after mixing a cake, rolling out and cutting pastry after the pie or tart has been made, running teeth over apple peelings for a taste of the fruit, licking a finger and dabbing at sifted icing sugar on a work surface are just a few of the perks of cooking with an adult. Of course, Milly-Molly-Mandy doesn't do anything as greedy as licking the wooden spoon, but in one memorable story she does make a wonderful little patty-pan cake with the leftovers of the cake mix.

In "Milly-Molly-Mandy Goes Sledging" she is desperate to go outside and play in the snow, but her parents think she should wait until it settles, so mother and daughter bake together. Milly-Molly-Mandy stands on a chair, deals with the sultanas, beats the eggs, and stirs the mix.

"And after Mother had filled the cake tins [she] was allowed to put the scrapings into her own little patty-pan and bake it for her own self in the oven (and that sort of cake always tastes nicer than any other sort, only there's never enough of it!)."

What is so appealing here is the miniature aspect of her cake – it's a little cake in a little pan for a little girl. And it's wonderful that Milly-Molly-Mandy is treated as a mini-cook and allowed to make a real, not a pretend, cake.

We don't hear the word patty pan much these days, but any small tin for making patties or pastries or cakes is a 'patty-pan'. I think in the case of a patty-pan cake, scale is all-important; the result must look like a scaled-down version of a larger cake, and not just like a small one. You can find dinky little baking tins in John Lewis or on the de Cuisine website (www.decuisine.co.uk) or you can use larger trays that are designed to make six or eight cakes of the same shape.

Although it's quite easy to give a child a little of whatever you are baking to make an individual little cake or tart or pudding, this recipe ensures there *is* enough mixture to satisfy a budding baker.

It is worth looking for fresh, pale, plump, sweet sultanas as they are the whole point of this cake. And if you want them to be really juicy, soak them in the orange juice overnight in a small bowl before you start on the recipe.

Makes 8–10 patty-pan cakes or 1 medium cake
175 g soft butter
175 g soft brown sugar
3 eggs
175 g self-raising flour
Finely grated zest and juice of ½ orange (unwaxed)
50 g ground almonds
200 g sultanas

8–10 patty-pans or small cake tins, greased with butter *or* 1 18-cm round cake tin, greased with butter and lined with baking parchment

1. Preheat the oven to 160°C/Gas Mark 3.
2. In a large mixing bowl, cream the butter and sugar until pale and fluffy. Beat in the eggs one at a time. Sift in the flour, add the orange zest, ground almonds, sultanas and orange juice and fold gently into the mix with a large metal spoon.
3. Spoon the mix into the patty-pans or cake tin(s), filling them two-thirds full. Allow plenty of 'leftovers' for bowl-scraping and spoon-licking.
4. Bake until the cakes are well risen and firm to the touch, and a skewer inserted into the centre of one of the cakes (or the large cake) comes out clean. Allow 25–30 minutes for little cakes and approximately 1–1½ hours for a large one. Exact baking times will vary according to the size of the patty-pans or cake tin(s).
5. Leave to cool on a wire rack in their tin(s) and turn out when cold.

Anne of Green Gables' Liniment Layer Cake

It is not all sweetness and light in the kitchens of classic children's stories. Sometimes bakers are fallible and dramatic disasters happen. And when they do, it's very reassuring for young readers whose own cakes may have collapsed to read about spectacular mishaps. So I would recommend that any budding baker read the chapter 'A New Departure in Flavourings' in *Anne of Green Gables* by L.M. Montgomery.

Lips are smacked by Anne and the reader alike as she describes to her best friend, Diana, the treats that have been prepared for the visit of the new minister and his wife (Anne's beloved Sunday School teacher):

"'We're going to have jellied chicken and cold tongue. We're to have two kinds of jelly, red and yellow, and whipped cream and lemon pie, and cherry pie, and three kinds of cookies, and fruit-cake, and Marilla's famous yellow-plum preserves that she keeps especially for ministers, and pound cake and layer cake, and biscuits as aforesaid.'"

The pièce de résistance is to be a layer cake made by Anne herself. It "comes out of the oven as light and feathery as golden foam" and Anne fills it with "layers of ruby jelly".

So it is mystifying when the gallantly polite Mrs Allan's peculiar expression suggests to Marilla that all is not as it should be with the layer cake. Sure enough, she discovers that Anne has flavoured the cake not with Best Vanilla but with Anodyne Liniment which Marilla had poured into an empty vanilla bottle.

Fortunately laughter, rather than serious food poisoning, follows, and it is heart-warming to be reminded that it's the 'kindness' and 'thoughtfulness' that go into the act of baking a cake that count more than anything. Something worth remembering when your well-intentioned efforts go horribly wrong.

The phrase 'layer cake' always makes me think of a cartoonishly huge, striped confection with lavish amounts of icing, which cut into toweringly slices at least 15 centimetres high. It is the epitome of generous, North American cooking, the kind of thing that would shock English cake-eaters more used to dainty little slices and bite-sized fondant fancies.

But a little research reveals that a layer cake is simply another way of describing any cake that has more than one layer and is sandwiched together with some sort of filling – cream, icing, jelly, curd, jam. However, I think any layer cake that emulates Anne's, but without the liniment, should be teeteringly tall and with some form of bright red filling.

My layer cake is a simple Victoria sponge sandwich, but for a four-layer cake I use double the usual quantities and bake the layers in two batches. This recipe makes a two-layer cake, so multiply everything by two if you are making a four-layer cake and give yourself plenty of time to do all the necessary baking and cooling before assembling it. For both versions, you can use more or less cream and strawberries for the filling and topping, according to taste.

MAKES 1 TWO-LAYER CAKE
250 g caster sugar
250 g soft butter
4 large eggs
250 g self-raising flour
A few drops of vanilla extract

FOR THE FILLING AND TOPPING:

1 medium (284 ml) carton double cream, whipped (1 large / 568 ml carton for
  a four-layer cake)
1 punnet strawberries, washed, hulled and sliced into halves or quarters
  (2 punnets for a four-layer cake)

2 21-cm round cake tins, greased with butter

1. Preheat the oven to 180°C/Gas Mark 4.
2. Cream the sugar and butter until pale and fluffy.
3. Beat in the eggs one at a time (add a tablespoonful of the flour with each
   addition if necessary to stop the mix curdling), together with the vanilla extract.
4. Sift in the flour and fold in with a large metal spoon.
5. Divide the mixture evenly between the two cake tins (use scales if you want to be
   really precise) and bake for 25 minutes or until the cakes are golden and firm, and
   a metal skewer or sharp knife inserted into the centre of one of them comes out
   clean.
6. Leave the cakes in their tins on a wire rack to cool, then turn them out.
7. Repeat the whole operation if you are making more than two layers.
8. Once the cakes are cool you can build up the layers. For a two-layer cake, place
   one of the sponges on the serving plate and spread half the whipped cream on top.
   Sprinkle half the strawberries evenly over the cream, then add the second sponge.
   Put the remaining cream and strawberries on the top of the cake.
9. For a four-layer cake, repeat the process with the remaining two sponges.

PAULINE'S ICED AND PATTERNED CAKES

You'd be forgiven for thinking from its title and various cover designs that *Ballet Shoes* by Noel Streatfeild is the ultimate girly book. And yet it turns out to be a wonderfully progressive and forward-thinking story of how the three young Fossil girls are allowed to develop their identities and interests naturally, and not in accordance with any social expectations. A frilly, frothy, pink satin and organdie extravaganza it most certainly is not.

Throughout the book it is Pauline who, by nature and not conditioning, is the most domestic, and she loves being in the kitchen or sewing or embroidering. So when she needs to be distracted from the prospect of her first matinee performance, Cook knows exactly what to do:

"She let Pauline do all the icing on the cakes... and let her squeeze names and patterns on them. She enjoyed herself so much and was so busy that she forgot all about the afternoon, and was amazed when Nana said it was time to wash for their lunch."

What a lovely way to describe the way children find baking so absorbing and creative that it helps them forget their anxieties and worries and concentrate on making something both delicious and pretty for a late tea.

The messages are clear. We should let our children develop their own natures, whether they are homebodies with ambitions to act (like Pauline), or future female aviators (like Petrova). And, of course, baking is good for you.

Here is a recipe for basic cakes (we call them fairy buns but to others they are cup-cakes). These are the perfect vehicle for all the therapeutic squeezing of icing and pattern-making a worried or anxious child or adult could need.

The cakes must be *completely* cool before you begin to ice them, otherwise the icing will melt and slip off. As for the colour, do not bother with liquid dyes. They make the icing runnier and give meagre colours. Even if it's the palest, pastel shade you are after, paste is best. I use pastes made by Squires or Sugarflair (see Resources, page 297) and a little goes a long, long way.

The recipe below is for an icing to cover buns. For patterns and writing you need to use Royal (Writing) Icing (see page 272) or, alternatively, buy the tubes of 'writing icing' that are available in supermarkets.

MAKES 12 ICED CAKES
125 g soft butter
125 g caster sugar
2 large eggs
A few drops of vanilla extract
    (optional)
125 g self-raising flour

FOR THE ICING:
250–330 g icing sugar
Juice of 2–3 lemons
Food-colouring paste

12-hole bun tray or muffin tin; 12 paper cases

1. Preheat the oven to 180°C/Gas Mark 4.
2. Place the paper cases in the holes in the tin.
3. In a large bowl, cream the butter and sugar with a wooden spoon or electric mixer until pale and fluffy.
4. Add the eggs and the vanilla, if using, and beat well to incorporate.
5. Sift in the flour and fold in gently with large metal spoon.
6. Divide the mix evenly between the cake cases.

7. Bake for 15–20 minutes until the tops are golden and firm. Leave to cool slightly on a wire rack before taking the cakes in their paper cases out of the tin.

8. To make the icing, start by sifting approximately 250 g of the icing sugar into a bowl.

9. Add about one-quarter of the lemon juice and a tiny amount of food-colouring paste on the end of a wooden cocktail stick that can then be thrown away. Mix well using a sturdy knife. Now add more lemon juice and/or paste until you happy with the consistency and colour.

10. Mix until you have a thick, glossy, evenly coloured icing that is spreadable but won't slide off the cakes.

11. Make sure the cakes are completely cold, then apply the icing generously in a swirling movement with a palette knife. You don't need to go right up to the edges of the buns as the icing will spread out a little.

12. When the icing has set you can decorate the cakes with patterns and writing.

UNCLE AMBROSE'S
STRAWBERRY JAM

I always appreciate a well-developed culinary motif. When I read of Winnie-the-Pooh and his honey, Paddington Bear and his marmalade sandwiches, Snubby and his meringues, and Richmal Crompton's William and his beloved gobstoppers, I know that all is right with a world in which a favourite and reassuring foodstuff makes an appearance at the perfect moment.

Elizabeth Goudge could not resist a food motif, either, and *Linnets and Valerians* is delightfully and deliciously underpinned by strawberry jam. It is the sticky undercurrent of the four children's relationship with their eccentric, scholarly Uncle Ambrose, with whom they propose to live after running away from their autocratic, non-strawberry-jam-offering grandmother.

Although he himself abhors strawberry jam and muffins, Uncle Ambrose asks his factotum, Ezra, to buy some for the children soon after they descend (unexpectedly) on him. This is the moment they realise that Uncle Ambrose likes them, and will let them live with him, for their childish but astute reasoning is, "Does a man buy muffins and jam for those whom he dislikes?"

The children also enjoy a tremendous strawberry jam-making session with Uncle Ambrose, who is the epitome of the intelligent rather than the instinctive cook – he believes he knows when jam reaches setting point simply because he possesses "sufficient intelligence to know when strawberries become jam". He takes over confidently from the not-very-intelligent but supremely gifted and intuitive cook Ezra, and he and the children all stir and watch until Robert yells, "The jam's jammed!" and a spoonful dropped on to a saucer sets like glue.

Uncle Ambrose's suspicion that it might be overcooked is confirmed when Ezra returns and harrumphs:

"'Huh,' said Ezra. ''Andsome is as 'andsome does an' come the morning there'll be no way o' getting that jam out o' them pots without takin' an 'atchet to them.'"

But the reader knows that the children have had a wonderful time with their uncle and have glimpsed an endearing fallibility, so even though the jam is rock hard, the process of learning and cooking together acts as a large blob of sticky, jammy glue that brings them together.

It is all too easy to overcook jam; the reason why so much jam turns out solid is that it is difficult for the first-time jam-maker to believe than such runny liquid will actually set when it cools. But if you test for setting point early on in the cooking process and trust your eyes, you shouldn't have any problems making a sweetly soft strawberry jam which is lovely on toast, Milly-Molly-Mandy's Muffin Man Muffins (page 56), Smashing Match Tea Jammy Buns (page 131) and Miss Dimity's Jam Scones (page 233). If you do cook it a little longer, it will simply turn out a little firmer.

MAKES 4 340-G JARS
1 kg strawberries
800 g granulated sugar
Juice of 1 lemon

4 340-g jars, washed and dried (see Step 1)

127

1. In advance of making the jam, wash the jars in hot, soapy water and rinse with very hot water. Allow them to dry, preferably in a cool (150°C/Gas Mark 2) oven, without touching the insides with your hands or a tea towel. Also, put 3–4 saucers in the freezer.

2. When you are ready, rinse and hull the strawberries. Pat with kitchen paper to remove excess liquid. You may want to cut the strawberries into halves or quarters depending on how big they are and the size of fruit you want in your jam.

3. Put the strawberries, sugar and lemon juice in a large pan with a heavy base.

4. Heat gently and stir now and again until the sugar has dissolved.

5. Bring to the boil and boil rapidly for up to 8–10 minutes, but start to test for setting point after 6–7 minutes. To do this, remove the pan from the heat, drop a teaspoonful of the liquid on to a cold saucer from the freezer, allow it to cool a little then push the edge with a finger. If the surface wrinkles, setting point has been reached. If not, return the pan to heat and continue boiling until the jam reaches setting point.

6. Remove the pan from the heat, place on a heatproof surface and skim off the scum with a large metal spoon. Allow the jam to cool in the pan for 20–30 minutes before pouring it into the warm, clean jars.

7. Cover with wax or cellophane discs and seal.

8. Once opened, this jam is best stored in the fridge.

SCHOOL
*F*OOD

W hen I say school food, I most definitely do not mean the food that is cooked in school kitchens and served in school dining halls. No, school food in this context means the lovely treats and sweetmeats that supplement the official diet in fictional schools, the foods that children import in tuck boxes, buy from the local sweet shops, order in from cake shops, or persuade parents to bring to speech days and picnics.

Without wanting to destroy too many illusions, though, I have to admit that while doing the research for this book I discovered that not all the famous schools in the stories are crammed with mouth-watering treats, tuck boxes and midnight feasts. It may appear to be that way when we look back fondly on our childhood reading, but on later, closer scrutiny we find that actually only a few writers are lavish with the details.

Angela Brazil, Antonia Forest and Anthony Buckeridge wrote dozens of school stories, but they rarely expended words and energy on working up the reader's

appetite. And I have noticed that the writers of boys' school stories are notably hearty and cavalier about food, which is all too often simply seen as fodder for active bodies. They have a disappointing tendency to gloss over meals, leaving the greedy, food-conscious reader somewhat hungry and unfulfilled.

So if it's food detail we want, we have to turn to the ever-reliable, feminine worlds of Enid Blyton, Elinor M. Brent-Dyer and American writers such as Jean Webster and Susan Coolidge, who have no reservations about gratifying the appetites of both characters and readers.

Of course, these fictional school treats are part of a greater fantasy that school days *will* be the happiest days of our lives, that we will all have super, smashing, topping educational experiences and that we will never have to deal with disgusting, bland, overcooked school dinners again. But the frequently very different reality never stopped a fan of this type of story from swallowing every sweet detail of school food as it could be in an ideal world.

For more school treats, see Voyages of Discovery Bunloaf (page 159); Very Nice Last Mouthful Cherry Cake (page 64); Debby's Jumbles (page 105); Paddington's Favourite Marmalade Buns (page 37); Turkish Delight (page 262); Aunt Fanny's Treacly, Sticky Ginger Cake (page 66).

Smashing Match Tea Jammy Buns

F elicity "went off with her team and the Wellsborough girls to a 'smashing' tea. Anyone seeing the piles of sandwiches, buttered and jammy buns, and slices of fruit cake would think that surely it would need twenty teams to eat all that!

But the two teams managed it all between then quite easily. What fun it all was! …

'School's smashing,' thought Felicity, munching her fourth jammy bun. 'Super! Wizard!'"

The Malory Towers books are pure, escapist pleasure. I never had any desire whatsoever to go to boarding school, but these wonderful books transported me to a parallel universe inhabited by girls called Gwendoline Mary and Zerelda Brass, French teachers with a sense of humour bypass, teachers nicknamed 'Jimmy', bossy girls and boastful girls and girls who are bricks, and girls whose vocabularies include 'smashing' and 'wizard' and 'super', and who are always frightfully pleased to be playing for the school lacrosse team.

To someone happily curled up and reading books indoors, lacrosse sounded like a cold, vicious game, but the idea of sucking sour lemons at half-time made my mouth water and, by the time it came to victory and the match tea — well, I might just have been persuaded to wield a lax stick simply to earn the right to eat a few jammy buns with Felicity and the rest of the team in *In the Fifth at Malory Towers*.

Jammy buns are one of those treats that appear in children's literature with almost comical, cartoonish regularity. They are the epitome of child-friendly food – appealingly round, sticky, colourful, and easy to eat. Yet I would hazard a guess that very few of us who read the kind of books in which wizard jammy buns are munched ever tasted a good, fresh, home-made, sweetened yeast bread with red jam squishing and oozing out of its centre.

So I want to remedy this omission by providing a recipe for classic, smashing jammy buns. These should be eaten in great quantities, fresh, split and jammed, after some hearty activity – real or fictitious.

When dusted with icing sugar and filled with jam and whipped cream, these buns are also known as Devonshire Splits, one of Marmaduke Saffron's specialities in *The Little White Horse*, and a classic English treat.

MAKES 18 BUNS

15 g or 1 dessertspoon dried yeast
1 teaspoon runny honey or caster sugar
430 ml milk
680 g strong white flour
15 g sea salt
110 g butter

Oil, for greasing
Icing sugar, for dusting
Strawberry or raspberry jam,
*   for filling*
Whipped cream, for filling (optional)

Large baking tray, lined with baking parchment

1. Put the yeast and honey or sugar in a bowl. Warm the milk until it is lukewarm (but not hotter) then pour it on to the yeast and sugar and stir well. Leave for a few minutes to make sure the yeast is alive and well. If the mix does not start to bubble or froth the yeast is not alive and you should start again with a fresh batch.
2. Sift the flour and salt into a large mixing bowl. Rub in the butter until the mixture resembles fine breadcrumbs. Make a well in the centre and pour in the liquid. Mix to a dough with your hand.
3. Turn out on to a floured work surface and knead for 5–8 minutes until the dough

is very smooth and elastic. Shape into a ball.

4. Lightly grease the mixing bowl with oil and return the dough to the bowl. Cover with clingfilm or a damp tea towel and leave the dough to rise until it has doubled in size. This will take 1½–2 hours depending on the temperature of the room.

5. When the dough has doubled in size, preheat the oven to 200°C/Gas Mark 6.

6. Knock back the dough, turn it out of the bowl on to a floured surface and knead lightly for 30 seconds.

7. Divide the dough into 18 equal pieces and roll them into balls. Arrange the balls on the baking tray so that they almost touch each other. Cover with oiled clingfilm or a damp tea towel and leave to rise for a further 30–45 minutes.

8. Bake for 20 minutes or until the buns are golden brown and sound hollow when tapped on the base.

9. Transfer the tray to a wire rack and dust the buns with icing sugar immediately.

10. Let the buns cool then make a cut diagonally through the top of each one with a breadknife, fill with strawberry or raspberry jam (and whipped cream, if desired) and serve straightaway.

Tuck-Box Treats

Tuck boxes must have a lot to answer for. I wonder how many children have wished to go to boarding school simply to experience the joys they bring, as portrayed in children's literature.

Fictional tuck boxes are an opportunity to indulge in the fantasy of having all the treats you've ever wished for in one box, of having a cache of food you can access when school food is dreary, when you need to curry favour with friends, or guarantee an invite to a midnight feast. Even the so-called boring or unimpressive tuck boxes of yore sound like lovely treats, and a delightful taste of home cooking to modern children who are more likely to have crisps, pot noodles and large bars of chocolate in theirs.

Take, for example, the tuck boxes that accompany Elizabeth, the Naughtiest Girl in the School, to Whyteleaf School. She despises their somewhat plain and wholesome contents, and endures agonies when she finds she can't compete with the gorgeous chocolate cakes, extravagant birthday cakes or lavish boxes of chocolates the other girls receive. And yet, to me, her tuck boxes sound lovely: jam sandwich cake, currant cake, golden syrup, tins of toffee, blackcurrant jam and shortbread.

There is clearly a well-defined hierarchy of literary tuck boxes, and for my money and peppermint creams, they do not come much better than the one received by Katy and Clover Carr when they have to spend Christmas at school in What Katy Did at School.

Katy's parents and their cook Debby pull out all the stops, to such an extent that the 'Carr's Box' passes into school legend as "as an example of what papas and mammas could accomplish, when they were of the right sort, and really wanted to make schoolgirls happy".

This is an edible Chinese box, apparently bottomless and filled with boxes within boxes. "Each box held a different kind of cake. One was full of jumbles, another of ginger-snaps; a third of crullers, and the fourth contained a big square loaf of frosted plum-cake, with a circle of sugar almonds set in the frosting." Then there are "parcels of figs, prunes, almonds, raisins, candy; under those, apples and pears". The tuck box is on such a scale that Katy and Clover can make little parcels of goodies, all beautifully wrapped, for each of their friends and still have the equivalent of Fortnum & Mason's food hall left over. It's all quite marvellous, and must have made many readers long to spend Christmas at school – for the tuck box alone.

There are a number of recipes in these pages for treats that do not need to be eaten immediately and would therefore be perfect in tuck boxes – or any box of treats, for that matter: Debby's Jumbles (page 105); Pippi Longstocking's Heart-Shaped Swedish Ginger Snaps (page 246); Great Fruit Cake (page 69); Bruce Bogtrotter's Heroic Chocolate Cake (page 249); Voyages of Discovery Bunloaf (page 159); Mrs Corry's Gilt Gingerbread (page 202); Cook's Special Sugar Biscuits (page 230); Loveday's Marriage Proposal Parkin (page 270); Milly-Molly-Mandy's Little Patty-Pan Sultana Cakes (page 117); Tempting Turkish Delight (page 262).

CHALET SCHOOL APPLE CAKE

A s a child I was encouraged to borrow rather than buy books, and I developed a serious library habit from a very early age. I can still remember arriving at my senior school and being flabbergasted by the number of wonderful books available for borrowing from the 'junior' library. Even now, in my mind's eye, I can see exactly where all the Chalet School stories were to be found; Elinor M. Brent-Dyer's series took up a huge amount of shelf space and I worked my way through every Chalet School title the school owned. Ah, the delights of addictive reading, wishing a series would never end, and seriously wanting to go to school in the Tyrol.

It amuses me to recall that I happily read all the German food references without understanding a word, and that this never once bothered me. 'Funny things' such as *Butterbrod, Pflaumenmarmelade, Kalbsbraten* and *Kartoffeln* simply added to the difference and to the excitement of going to school in Austria; it was as if the idea of the strange foods mattered more than the foodstuffs themselves. As long as it was all 'simply ripping' and 'topping', I wasn't going to let the matter of a little German vocabulary put me off.

Occasionally, however, there was a helpful translation of a particular treat which only served to whet my appetite further. So in *The School at the Chalet* we are told that *Apfeltorte* isn't an apple tart, but a "sort of cake with cooked apples on it". Mmmm, this is irresistible, and the minute I read this I am whisked away to a little Austrian *Gasthaus* where each of the boisterous Chalet School girls is enjoying a large slice of cake with a cup of the "excellent coffee" that everyone drinks throughout the book.

What a stroke of genius: locating a school in a country where coffee and cakes, or *Kaffe und Küchen*, are a way of life. No wonder pupils flocked to join.

136

This is my easy-to-make interpretation of *Apfeltorte*. I am making no claims to authenticity, except to say that it includes ingredients that are frequently used in Austrian baking, such as apples, hazelnuts and cinnamon.

Makes 1 medium cake (serves 6–8)
100 g self-raising flour
½ teaspoon ground cinnamon or a good grating of nutmeg
100 g hazelnuts
1 unwaxed lemon
3–4 apples (Cox or Granny Smith)
125 g soft butter, plus 25 g melted butter
125 g soft brown sugar
3 eggs
2 tablespoons milk
Caster sugar, for sprinkling
Whipped cream, to serve

20-cm round spring-form or loose-bottomed cake tin, greased with butter and lined with baking parchment

1. Preheat the oven to 180°C/Gas Mark 4.
2. Sift the flour and cinnamon or nutmeg into a bowl. Grind the hazelnuts but be careful not to over-grind them because they will turn oily – and, anyway, a little nutty texture is fine in this cake. Add the nuts to the bowl. Grate the zest of the lemon into the flour and nuts (don't throw away the lemon), and stir in gently.
3. Peel and slice the apples quite thinly (they need to cook fully during baking). Place in a bowl and squeeze a little of the juice from the lemon over them as you go along to stop them turning brown.

4. In a large mixing bowl, cream the softened butter and the soft brown sugar. Beat in the eggs one at a time. Add the flour, nut and spice mix, and the milk and fold in gently.

5. Spoon into the tin and level the surface with the back of a metal spoon.

6. Arrange the apple slices on top and brush with the melted butter. Sprinkle caster sugar evenly over the apples.

7. Bake for 35–40 minutes until a metal skewer or sharp knife inserted in the middle of the cake comes out clean.

8. Leave the cake in its tin on a wire rack to cool for 10–15 minutes, then remove the cake from the tin.

9. Serve warm with whipped cream and coffee, and a stack of Chalet School books from the library. Alternatively, gather together a group of Chalet School lovers and serve as part of a *Kaffe und Küchen* celebration.

Judy's Educational
Molasses Candy Pull

O h, the joy of finding a wonderfully readable and romantic novel when you are on the cusp of adolescence. A novel whose orphaned heroine is lovable, natural and definitely not perfect, who writes funny and clever letters to a romanti‑ cally mysterious benefactor, and who immerses herself in all aspects of her education: academic, sentimental and practical. I don't think there are many books that could replace Judy and *Daddy‑Long‑Legs* in my formative reading, and I can still recall the copious tears that were shed at the end.

One of my favourite letters written by Judy to Daddy‑Long‑Legs describes a molasses candy pull organised during the Christmas holidays for the students who are left behind in the college. The girls all troop into the huge kitchen in their white caps and aprons and proceed to boil and then pull the toffee until it is pale and firm. The results leave the kitchen, doorknobs and students sticky and the professors to whom the candy is offered, speechless. But the process is deemed great fun by Judy: "So you see, Daddy, my education progresses!" she writes.

Having no idea of the meaning of the words, the process or the results, I was mystified by the idea of a candy pull, but the suggestion of having fun with your friends making sticky, sugary stuff appealed enormously. It was only while doing the research for this book that I discovered that candy, or taffy, pulls were (and, in some places, still are) great social events for young people, particularly in the east of America where the winters are long and cold, and where any activity in a warm kitchen is to be welcomed.

Molasses and sugar are boiled and, as soon as the hot toffee can be held, it is pulled and pulled until it is cool and hard. This can be done by individuals or in pairs, and the strands can be shaped as you please (twists, whirls, rounds or even romantic, entwining initials) then wrapped individually in cellophane or greaseproof paper.

A candy pull makes an excellent winter activity for older children who can be trusted with handling relatively hot toffee, and it works brilliantly at parties as long as all the cooks don aprons, tie their hair back and grease their hands. And bear in mind that no matter how messy and sticky everything and everyone gets, it's all educational.

MAKES ENOUGH FOR 4 PEOPLE TO HAVE A MOLASSES CANDY PULL (APPROX. 250 G FINISHED CANDY)

225 g molasses sugar or soft dark brown sugar
2 tablespoons molasses or treacle
2 tablespoons cider or white wine vinegar
½ teaspoon baking soda
Butter, for greasing hands

Baking tray, greased with butter; sugar thermometer

1. Place the baking tray on a wire rack. Have a a couple of small bowls of ice-cold water at the ready for testing the candy.
2. Place all the ingredients except the baking soda in a deep, heavy pan. Bring to the boil, stirring constantly with a wooden spoon.
3. Lower the heat to medium and cook, without stirring, for approximately 8 minutes or until the temperature reaches 124°C; or until a small amount of syrup

dropped in cold water separates into hard but pliable threads that do not stick to fingers. Be vigilant at this point as the candy mix can start to burn very suddenly.

4. Remove the pan from the heat and place on a heatproof surface.

5. Now quickly dissolve the baking soda in a teaspoon of cold water and add to the molasses mixture (it will foam immediately). Stir well with a wooden spoon, then pour the candy on to the baking tray and leave to cool on the wire rack for 5 minutes.

6. With a metal spatula, fold the edges of the candy over towards the centre. Repeat until an indentation remains after the surface is poked and the mixture is cool enough to be handled.

7. With buttered hands, gather the candy into a ball and begin to pull. It's easy enough for one person to do this on their own, but it's even more entertaining when you work in pairs. Pull the candy into a rope, fold it in half and twist the strands together. Continue pulling, folding and twisting until the candy is glossy and lightly streaked throughout; this will take about 5 minutes. If the candy breaks just keep putting it back together and pulling. When it is cool and semi-firm, pull and twist it evenly into a rope 1 cm thick. Place on a work surface.

8. With scissors dipped in cold water, cut the rope into 2½ cm pieces, working quickly while the candy is still supple. Layer between greaseproof paper (don't let the pieces touch or they will stick together).

9. Store in airtight container for up to two weeks.

AMY'S PICKLED LIMES

Food crazes in schools are nothing new, but they can be mystifying to those who weren't there at the time. However the craze for pickled limes has passed into legend, thanks to Amy March's passion for them in *Little Women* (1868), and they have continued to intrigue many generations of readers. Indeed, Judy in *Daddy-Long-Legs* (1912) takes steps to discover what the fuss is about after finding it difficult to understand other students' references to pickled limes when she arrives at her new college:

"I find I am the only girl in college who wasn't brought up on *Little Women*. I haven't told anybody though… I just went and bought it with $1.12 of my last month's allowance; and the next time somebody mentions pickled limes, I'll know what she's talking about."

It's funny that this 'contraband article', the pickled lime, still makes mouths water when mentioned in *Little Women*, and I particularly like the image of all those apparently sweet young ladies sucking on sour limes at their desks during lessons and then trading them for trinkets, favours, party invitations and general popularity at recess. When Amy is undone by her lime-debts and lime-favours it's as if this squeeze of lime juice is just what's needed to cut through the sugariness of her self-image and conceit, and the limes are used as a wonderfully tart metaphor.

Pickled limes sound so alluring and appetising – particularly to contemporary readers who are currently in the middle of a fashion for sour sweets. Sourness holds a strange appeal for children, who have always loved treats such acid drops, lemon sherbets and sour plums with their underlying streak of acidity which counteracts the sweetness and creates a daring flavour to excite youthful palates. It seems that pickled limes were simply an early forerunner of this slightly masochistic indulgence;

Key limes, pickled in saltwater and shipped from Florida to Boston, were a popular snack with schoolchildren in the east of America in the mid-nineteenth century.

Taking my cue from the element of salt in the originals, I am giving this recipe for what I call Amy's pickled limes, but others may prefer to call them preserved limes. Today the phrase 'pickled limes' tends to mean a spicy condiment in which the limes are cooked with spices and oil, whereas preserved limes are similar to whole, preserved lemons that are prepared without any cooking and using just salt and juice.

MAKES 1 500-ML JAR
5–6 fresh, unblemished, unwaxed limes (enough to fill the jar when pressed down)
Fine salt

500 ml sealable jar, washed and sterilised

1. Wash and dry the limes.
2. With a sharp knife, make four deep incisions from top to bottom in each lime. Take care not to cut right through the limes – they need to stay in one piece.
3. Pour a few tablespoons of salt into a bowl. Hold each lime over the bowl and gently press on the ends of the lime to open it up, one slit at a time. Press as much salt as you can into each slit and roll the lime in salt. Place in the jar.
4. Repeat the process for each lime and pack as many limes into the jar as possible.
5. Close the jar and shake well.
6. Leave for a week in a cool place. Shake the jar each day to disperse the liquid and salt. After the first week store the limes in the fridge.
7. Eat, suck, or use in cooking.

MARVELLOUS
MIDNIGHT FEASTS

When it comes to midnight feasts, one fictional school for girls stands head and shoulders above the rest: Enid Blyton's St Clare's. While Whyteleaf School (where Elizabeth is the Naughtiest Girl in the School) ranks second, and Malory Towers is the place for outdoorsy, sporty types who can eat for the school after lacrosse and swimming, St Clare's is *the* place for illicit feasts. Matron here can even diagnose 'Midnight Feast Illness' and some feasts pass into school legend, such as the one to celebrate Janet's birthday in *The Twins at St Clare's* which consists of chocolate cake, shortbread, sardines and Nestle's milk, supplemented by ginger beer, chocolate, cake, pork pie and peppermint creams.

The very best midnight feasts generally feature an unusual location, a select list of guests and an outlandish combination of food. So Carlotta's feast in *The Second Form at St Clare's* is a mix of sweet and savoury, fishy and fruity – often in the same mouthful. She opens the box provided by grandmother and exclaims,

"'Sardines! And what's this – an *enormous* tin of pineapple chunks... Bars of chocolate-cream... Enough to feed the whole school I should think!... Tins of prawns. I say – I do like prawns. Golly – prawns and pineapple – what a heavenly mixture that would be.'"

When it comes to the feast itself, "Carlotta even ate pineapples and sardines together. Alison tried prawns dipped in ginger beer" and Janet is thrilled with her new discovery: "Nobody would dream that sardines pressed into gingerbread cake would taste so nice... My brother told me that – and I didn't believe him. But it's true.'"

However, my favourite feast is the one held to celebrate Tessie's birthday in *The*

O'Sullivan Twins. This is the one that takes midnight feasts to new heights of daring and culinary excitement; as Winnie tells Tessie, "I don't believe ANYONE has ever fried sausages at a birthday party in the middle of the night before!... It would be a most marvellous thing to do."

So the guests all crowd into the music room and cook sausages on a borrowed oil stove – to go with fruit cake, ginger cake, sweets, biscuits and home-made toffee and tinned peaches and Nestle's cream. Until the non-invited Erica sneaks on them and they are discovered *in flagrante delicto* by a horrified Mam'zelle.

Fortunately Miss Theobald, the headmistress, is a brick and merely stops them going into town for a fortnight in search of more acceptable eating excitement. After all, she needs to maintain St Clare's position at the top of the midnight feast table.

HOW TO ORGANISE YOUR OWN MIDNIGHT FEAST

- Invites: Whisper the invitation to the guests 24 hours in advance
- When: Midnight, on the dot
- Set: Your alarm clock

- Where: A location where you won't be discovered (music room, common room, dormitory)
- Catering: Large hamper delivered by a relative
- Cake: Order a huge one with iced roses and candles
- What to bring: Each guest makes a contribution from his/her tuck box to maximise possibilities for strange food combinations
- Dress: Dressing gown and slippers
- Security: Close curtains/blinds and place pillows/cushions at the bottom of doors so teachers won't see the light
- Borrow: Oil stove for frying sausages
- Don't: Tell your worst enemy, cook kippers or burn the sausages
- Back to bed: When everything has been eaten
- Next day: Don't let Matron see that you feel ill, or she'll dose you

The Adventurous Life

What is the ultimate fantasy of freedom and independence when you are a child? A parent-free summer? A holiday under canvas? A sailing adventure? Joining the circus? Living in a caravan? It's so hard to choose that I'm sure many a young suburban reader (like I was) has found herself reading books throughout her entire school holidays so that she can investigate all the possibilities and enjoy them vicariously.

The freedom-seeking reader will discover a rich seam of adventure books published in the 1930s and 1940s. In these decades there is a rather alarming tendency for parents to disappear or to abandon their children in the school holidays, thus forcing them to become self-sufficient and self-reliant. Of course, this makes for marvellous tales with excellent descriptions of camp- and caravan- and boat-cooking, even though we now know that the reality of this need to keep calm, cope and carry on was rooted in the more depressing circumstances of the threat, and eventually the reality, of a world war and the experiences of rationing and evacuation.

The fact remains, however, that stories of camping and caravanning and

maritime adventures, with or without adults, are perennial favourites and are no doubt responsible for generation of children *and* adults wanting to hit the road or sail away with a bunloaf and a tin of cocoa.

The recipes that follow include several stalwarts of the small-scale dwelling and outdoor living experience. They are easy to make, easy to transport, easy to eat.

For more treats suitable for outdoor living see Creamy Porridge (page 16); Wake-Up-and-Smell-the-Breakfast with Hash Browns (page 18); Great Fruit Cake (page 69); Diana's Favourite Fruity Fruit Cake (page 72); Lashings of Hard-Boiled Eggs (page 171); Dickon's Roasted Eggs (page 174); Seven Little Australians' Damper (page 182); Aunt Fanny's Treacly, Sticky Ginger Cake (page 66); Loveday's Marriage Proposal Parkin (page 270).

MATE SUSAN'S
SCRAMBLED EGGS

V ery occasionally a children's author will give a wonderfully detailed descrip-tion of how to cook something. For many children, this might be their first encounter with a 'recipe', so it's all the more vital that the writer makes the process sound manageable, and the end result sound tasty. Arthur Ransome, a stickler for realistic detail, is particularly good at this and, as his books promote self-sufficiency in children, he makes sure they are able to cook something good, wholesome and simple. And what could be easier and tastier than scrambled eggs straight from the pan?

In the first expedition in *Swallows and Amazons*, Roger, John, Susan and Titty set up camp in a lovely spot and, after exploring the island, return to their base for supper. The fire is burning merrily, the kettle is boiling and Susan decides to make scrambled eggs. It's time for the reader to pay attention:

First she melts a big pat of butter in the frying pan and cracks six raw eggs on the edge of a mug and breaks them into a pudding-basin.

She then empties the raw eggs into the sizzling butter, and stirs the eggs and the butter together after shaking the pepper pot over them, and putting in plenty of salt.

Titty, who has observed Mrs Jackson scrambling eggs, advises her that as soon as they begin to flake, she must keep scraping them off the bottom of the pan.

And that's it, the eggs are scrambled, and the pan is set down on the ground and all four children tuck in from the "common dish" because "egg's awful stuff for sticking to plates".

With huge slices of brown bread and butter, and mugs of tea, scrambled eggs make an unparalleled camp-fire meal. Easy to make, easy to eat and, if you use a non-stick pan, easy to wash up.

A FEW FINER POINTS OF EGG-SCRAMBLING

1. Use large free-range eggs that are at room temperature.
2. Allow 2 eggs for one person, 3–4 eggs for two people, 6–8 eggs for four people, and so on.
3. Have your bread sliced and buttered, or ready to toast before you start scrambling.
4. Break each egg into a small bowl before putting it into a large bowl. This way, you can check that each egg is fresh and remove any pieces of eggshell. Don't add any liquid such as milk as it will turn the eggs watery. Once all your eggs are in one bowl, add salt and pepper and mix lightly with a whisk or fork before transferring them to a frying pan.
5. Cook the eggs over a low heat. The slower the cooking process the better. Use a wooden spatula to stir, turn and 'scrape'.
6. Remove the eggs when they have almost reached the consistency you like; they will continue to cook for a short time in the pan.
7. Put the pan in hot, soapy water as soon as you've finished. Titty's right – eggs are awful stuff for sticking.

Sausages and Spangles, Cocoa and Caravans

The first full-length, non-illustrated book I ever read on my own was Mr Galliano's Circus *by Enid Blyton. I was completely enthralled by the experience of reading independently and I devoured it in what felt like one sitting. This was the book that got me hooked on reading and on the delights of being whisked away to another world by the power of the printed word, plus it made me fall in love with the idea of living in a caravan.*

Jimmy Brown and his mother and his father all join the circus and move into a sweet little caravan provided by Mr Galliano. It's green on the outside and has matching green wheels with yellow spokes. The chimney is a cheerful yellow, as are the windowsills, while the interior is cream and the curtains are green and yellow. I wanted to live in the Browns' caravan so much, and to this day I still harbour a fondness for yellow, green and cream colour schemes.

And I wanted to sit on the steps of the caravan with Jimmy and Lotta (in her spangly acrobat's outfit) and eat sausages and potatoes in their skins, cooked on Mrs Brown's camp fire, followed by oranges and cocoa. It never occurred to me that they could be eating up the food from the circus acts; the clowns might have been stealing those strings of sausages before they were cooked and the jugglers could have been juggling in the ring with the hot potatoes or oranges.

*After the three Mr Galliano books, I moved on to the Famous Five and particularly adored the stories in which the children spend whole holidays in boys' and girls' caravans (*Five Go Off in a Caravan *and* Five Have a Wonderful Time*). I wanted to know every detail of the housekeeping and catering, and would willingly have swapped places with Anne, who revels in the responsibility of being the cook and does some magnificent bacon-and-egg fry-ups, although I would have have had to insist on more help with the washing-up.*

I've stayed in caravans since and it has never been quite as magical as I'd imagined, but that doesn't matter. The treat for me as a child was the opportunity to luxuriate in the possibilities a book could suggest. The possibility of escapism, of living in a small mobile dwelling, of frying sausages outside and baking potatoes in the embers of the fire, the possibility of contrasting bohemian company and tidy caravans, sausages and spangles, life on the road and the cosiness of a caravan. Let's not forget that one of the classic treats of childhood is not edible. It's a good book.

SWALLOWS AND
AMAZONS SEED CAKE

Every young explorer needs a good supply of seed cake. It's the talismanic food that makes regular appearances in the Swallows and Amazons stories and, by all accounts, it travels brilliantly.

In the second book of the series, *Swallowdale*, it is practically indestructible. After the *Swallow* sinks, John dives into the water to rescue the seed cake which Peggy then carefully dries out. Chief cook Susan thinks it can't be salvaged, but they soldier on with their adventures and eventually decide to fry slices of the cake when they get hungry and Susan is proved wrong.

As a result of its hardiness, Roger, Susan, John and Titty make sure they take a seed cake with them wherever they go. Thus, as many generations of young readers have discovered, this apparently boring cake acquires a whole new image when storybook children eat big slabs of it for supper with mugs of tea and apples to follow, or as part of a breakfast of eggs, bread, marmalade, bunloaf and bananas.

Seed cake is clearly a most marvellous substance, and yet we rarely eat it today. It may be something to do with the taste of caraway seeds (a little like fennel or liquorice) or with its simplicity and plainness (seed cake is simply a flavoured Madeira cake) or maybe it's the image of fusty dryness, but it has fallen out of fashion, together with tea-time and letting children sail away without adults. But all these things are worth reconsidering, and a well-made, fresh seed cake is a great cake for the outdoors as well as for genteel teas.

This recipe makes an ultra-traditional seed cake, caraway seeds and all. You can substitute poppy seeds if you wish, but that won't give the true taste of an English culinary and literary classic.

For adults, freshly baked seed cake is excellent served at 11 a.m. with a glass of Madeira. For children, it makes a wonderful picnic elevenses with home-made Easy-Peasy Lemon-Squeezy Lemonade (see page 190) or Gorgeous Ginger Beer (see page 193).

MAKES 1 MEDIUM CAKE (SERVES 6–8)
1 orange (unwaxed)
185 g soft butter
185 g caster sugar
3 eggs
150 g self-raising flour, sifted
125 g plain flour, sifted
2 teaspoons caraway seeds

18-cm round cake tin or medium loaf tin, greased with butter and lined with baking parchment

1. Preheat the oven to 160°C/Gas Mark 3.
2. Finely grate the orange zest and reserve it. Squeeze the orange to obtain the juice.
3. In a large mixing bowl, cream the butter and sugar until pale and fluffy, and beat in the eggs one at a time. With a large metal spoon, fold in the flours, caraway seeds, orange zest and 2–3 tablespoons of the orange juice.
4. Spoon the mix into the tin and flatten gently with the back of the spoon.
5. Bake for 1¼– 1½ hours until a metal skewer or sharp knife inserted in the cake comes out clean. Check after an hour; if the cake is browning too quickly, place a sheet of foil over it to prevent burning.
6. Leave in its tin on a wire rack to cool for 10–15 minutes, then turn out.

TINNED PINEAPPLE CAKE

Enid Blyton knows children are not inclined to be subtle when inventing names and nicknames. So in *Five Run Away Together* she calls the mean, thin, sour-faced cook who replaces the fat, generous Joanna at Kirrin Cottage 'Mrs Stick'. As a result, the reader is not surprised when Mrs Stick locks up the larder, hoards the best food for the decidedly dodgy Stick family, and even attempts to poison Timmy the dog.

At this point (and despite Julian's brave attempts to stand up to the Sticks and appropriate some decent food) they do what any self-respecting group of unsupervised children would do, and run away to Kirrin Island. But first they must prepare their provisions. Luckily, Mother has a store cupboard full of tins so they can stock up on tinned soup, fruit, milk, butter, sardines, vegetables and meat, and supplement these with bread, cake and, of course, bottles of ginger beer.

Tinned meals never sounded so good. Here is a "simply grand meal", the first they eat in their warm cave on the island:

"They opened a tin of meat, cut huge slices of bread and made sandwiches. Then they opened a tin of pineapple chunks and ate those, spooning them out of the tin, full of sweetness and juice."

Two tins of sardines eaten with biscuits follow, and Dick wonders, "My word, why don't people always have meals like this?"

Children are also not subtle about eating from tins, and with her careful choice of simple but evocative words Enid Blyton manages to make tinned pineapple the *ne plus ultra* of fine, island cuisine. The chunks with their juicy sweetness and mouth-watering acidity are delicious straight from the tin, or they can be used to make a really wonderful upside-down pineapple cake that is perfect for runaways to

take with them on a parent-free adventure. When you prepare the cake tin, make sure you grease the base very generously with butter as this will allow the pineapple rings to caramelise during baking.

MAKES 1 LARGE CAKE (SERVES 8–10)

175 g light soft brown sugar, plus extra (approx. 25 g) for sprinkling

1 x 432 g tin of 8 pineapple rings in fruit juice (not syrup)

8–16 whole glacé cherries (optional)

175 g soft butter

3 Eggs

150 g self-raising flour

½ teaspoon baking powder.

50 g ground almonds

Pineapple juice (from the tin)

50 g caster sugar

22-cm round spring-form cake tin, greased with butter

1. Preheat the oven to 180°C/Gas Mark 4.
2. Sprinkle about 25 g soft brown sugar over the generously buttered base of the cake tin.
3. Drain the pineapple rings, reserving the juice, and arrange them in the cake tin. Place a glacé cherry in the centre of each ring, if desired, and, if you wish, make a pretty pattern with more cherries.
4. Now make the sponge. In large mixing bowl, cream the butter and soft brown sugar until pale and fluffy. Beat in the eggs one at a time. Sift in the flour and baking powder, add the ground almonds and 2 tablespoons of the pineapple juice, and fold in gently with a metal spoon.
5. Spoon the mixture over the pineapple rings in the tin, level the surface with the back of the spoon, and bake for 40 minutes or until a metal skewer or sharp knife inserted in the cake comes out clean.
6. Leave the cake in its tin on a wire rack to cool for 10 minutes. While you are waiting, make a syrup by putting 100 ml pineapple juice and the caster sugar in a pan and boiling until it thickens. Remove from the heat.
7. Release the cake from the tin and turn it out on to a large, flat plate so that it is upside down with the pineapple rings on top. Pour the syrup evenly over the surface. Leave to cool completely before serving.

Voyages of
Discovery Bunloaf

When you enter the world of Arthur Ransome's children's books, life takes on all kinds of imaginative possibilities. A little lake can become a universe in which streams are rivers, hills are mountains, and islands are transformed into whole continents. This fiction also extends to food and drink; in *Swallows and Amazons* and *Swallowdale* even the most ordinary comestibles become exciting and exotic with overtones of piratical and smuggling adventures. So toffee is "molasses", lemonade is "Jamaica rum" or "grog", corned beef is "pemmican", and perch becomes "shark".

But there is one thing the children eat while sailing under the stars or camping out on their island that has always intrigued readers, despite the fact that it bears a thoroughly ordinary name, and this is bunloaf. We come across bunloaf packed in knapsacks together with apples, tea, sugar, milk, chocolate, toffees and "pemmican", or in picnic provisions with seed cake and bread and eggs, and it is probably the big hunk of black, juicy, sticky fruit cake that the Swallows and Amazons eat in *Swallowdale* ("enough for twelve indoor people and just right for six sailors").

In fact, this treat deserves a far more evocative name than the somewhat prosaic 'bunloaf' because it is actually the perfect accompaniment to the sailing adventures set in the Lake District. A rich, moist, spicy fruit loaf, it is a speciality of the Isle of Man and the Cumbrian coast, and the recipe dates back to the time when these places were the haunts of smugglers who brought in spices and spirits and tobacco. So it is an easy leap of the imagination from simple fruit loaf to something suffused with a spicy, swashbuckling history. It's just a shame that 'bunloaf' is such a misnomer.

This makes a large cake that is perfect for picnics and camping, and is easily sufficient for a dozen pirates/smugglers/sailors or a dozen or so 'indoor people'.

MAKES 1 LARGE CAKES (SERVES 12)

340 g plain flour	150 g sultanas
1 teaspoon mixed spice	125 g mixed peel
¼ nutmeg	1 tablespoon treacle
140 g butter	1 x 284 ml carton buttermilk
170 g soft brown sugar	1 teaspoon bicarbonate of soda
150 g currants	1 tablespoon milk, if necessary

Large (25 x 11 x 7) loaf tin, greased with butter and lined with baking parchment

1. Preheat the oven to 160°C/Gas Mark 3. *150°*

2. Sift the flour and mixed spice into a large mixing bowl and grate the nutmeg over the flour.

3. Rub the butter into the flour until it is all incorporated and the mixture looks like fine breadcrumbs.

4. Stir in the sugar and the dried fruit and mixed peel.

5. In another bowl, mix the treacle with the buttermilk and stir in the bicarbonate of soda, then add this to the mixing bowl. With a large spoon mix to a soft consistency, adding a little milk if the mixture seem too dry.

6. Spoon into the tin and bake in the oven for 2–2¼ hours until a metal skewer or sharp knife inserted in the centre of the cake comes out clean. Do not worry if the cake sinks a little in the middle – this is normal.

7. Leave the cake in its tin on a wire rack to cool, then turn out. Wrap in foil.

The Swallows'
Squashed-Fly Biscuits

B ritish biscuits have their very own subculture, one which no doubt perplexes other nations who find it hard to understand our fondness for discussions of the finer points of ginger nuts, digestives and custard creams. We also have some decidedly strange names for our favourite biscuits – jammy dodgers, Jaffa cakes, lemon puffs – but none so strange as the 'squashed-fly' biscuit.

The squashed-fly biscuit is the schoolboy name for the extremely flat Garibaldi biscuit whose layer of currants resembles the dead insects. It's been around since the nineteenth century, making young wags feel ineffably witty when they call it a 'fly cemetery' or a 'dead fly biscuit' or a 'fly sandwich'. Arthur Ransome plays on the joke in *Swallows and Amazons* when he includes some in the hamper that Mother brings to the children on the island.

As well as transporting an entire feast to celebrate baby Vicky's birthday, she also brings some "more ordinary stores" including, "a tin of golden syrup, two pots of marmalade and a great tin of squashed-fly biscuits. Squashed-fly biscuits are those flat biscuits with currants in, just the thing for explorers".

In fact, squashed-fly biscuits do have impeccable exploring credentials as Ransome, a former journalist, would have known. Ernest Shackleton took one ton of Garibaldi and ginger-nut biscuits on his 1907 British Antarctic Nimrod Expedition. So they are just the thing for young explorers who want to emulate the great Edwardian role models (the children in Ransome's books also refer to tinned meat as "pemmican", the staple, high-energy food of Scott's expeditions). Come fair weather or foul, you can always rely on a Great British Biscuit.

Even readers who are already familiar with squashed-fly biscuits will probably only ever have tasted those from packets, manufactured by such illustrious names as Huntley & Palmers, Peak Freans and Crawfords. But to be generous to non-British readers, and in the spirit of international cooperation, I think it's only right that I should give a recipe for home-made Garibaldi or squashed-fly biscuits. They may not be as hard-wearing as the branded type, but they are still perfect for food explorers.

Please don't think about using dried fruit other than currants; nothing else will work quite so effectively as a 'squashed-fly'.

MAKES 10–12 BISCUITS

200 g self-raising flour

Pinch of salt

100 g soft butter

125 g caster sugar, plus extra for sprinkling

2–3 tablespoons milk

1 egg, beaten

150 g currants

Baking tray, lined with baking parchment

1. Preheat the oven to 180°C/Gas Mark 4.
2. Sift the flour and salt into a large bowl and add the butter, sugar and 2 tablespoons of milk.
3. Mix all these ingredients with a wooden spoon, fork or by hand until it forms a smooth dough. Add a little more milk if the mixture is dry and crumbly.
4. Turn on to a well-floured work surface and roll out to form a large rectangle approximately 3 mm thick.
5. Brush some of the egg over the surface of the dough. With a sharp knife, cut

down the centre of the dough to make two equal rectangles.

6. Spread the currants over one half and press them down lightly with your hand. Using a large fish slice to pick up the dough, place the second half, egg-brushed side down, on top to form a sandwich. Press down again with the rolling pin.

7. Lightly brush the whole surface with more of the egg and sprinkle with caster sugar. Slice into squares or rectangles and transfer these to the baking tray.

8. Bake for 12–15 minutes until firm and pale gold.

9. Transfer the tray to a wire rack and leave the biscuits to cool.

10. Pack the biscuits in explorers' kits or serve with tea and chat about the merits of British biscuits.

CAMP-FIRE COCOA

No matter how often it is drunk in literature, the mere mention of cocoa never fails to make everything better. Cocoa flows through hundreds of twentieth-century children's books – warming, comforting, cheering, hot, steaming, sweet, milky, always welcome, always delicious whether sipped under the stars or next to a fire, at a kitchen table or on a school bench, for breakfast, dinner, tea or supper. Books contain huge jugs of steaming cocoa, camp-fire cocoa, supper cocoa, caravan cocoa, cave cocoa, picnic cocoa, cocoa made with water, cocoa made with milk, cocoa sweetened with condensed milk or sugar, and cocoa enriched with a spoonful of cream.

Of all the cocoas I have come across, the one that stands out is the camp-fire cocoa in *The Secret of Spiggy Holes* by Enid Blyton. The children have everything they need for a perfect cocoa moment: a secret island, a dry night, soft heather, warm blankets and a rabbit-skin rug, a cheerful fire, kettle, and even a source of fresh spring water. Peggy is the cocoa expert and makes it with water and cocoa, adding tinned milk and sugar afterwards, and it's enjoyed with biscuits, tomato soup, bread and a wonderful atmosphere. Cocoa, and life, don't get much better than this.

There's a vast difference between the indulgent, luxurious hot chocolate that is now in vogue, and the traditional, rather plain cocoa. Much as I like the occasional tiny cup of the former, I find cocoa far more drinkable and better suited to everyday occasions.

I'm giving two versions here; the first replicates the Spiggy Holes camp-fire cocoa made with tinned milk, and the second is a cocoa made with fresh milk. When we tested these, Phoebe and I were amazed at just how delicious steaming hot cocoa can be, and the cocoa made with evaporated milk was a revelation.

CAMP-FIRE COCOA I
Serves 6
Boiling water
1 tin good-quality cocoa powder
1 x 170 g tin evaporated milk
Sugar, to taste

1. While the kettle is boiling, place 1½–2 teaspoons cocoa in each of six mugs.
2. Pour on the boiling water and stir well.
3. Add the milk and sugar, and serve immediately.

CAMP-FIRE COCOA II

Makes 1 mug

2 teaspoons sugar, or to taste
1 tablespoon good-quality cocoa powder
Enough milk to fill the mug (approx. 150–180 ml)

1. Put the sugar and cocoa into a small pan with 2 tablespoons water. Heat gently and stir until smooth.
2. Allow the mix to boil for few seconds only, then slowly add the milk stirring constantly.
3. Pour into the mug and serve very hot.

PICNIC
TREATS

Hard-boiled eggs with a screw of salt. Freshly picked raspberries and ripe plums and rosy apples. Tomato sandwiches, potted meat sandwiches and cress sandwiches. Bottles of lemonade and ginger beer. New bread and butter and leftover jam tarts. Cool lettuce and freshly pulled radishes. Thick slices of fruit cake wrapped up in paper, packets of biscuits and bars of chocolate.

How well children's books capture the essence of a good picnic. Take what's available and plenty of it, use up leftovers, pick whatever is ready to be picked in the garden, make a few sandwiches, pack it all in a hamper, knapsack, satchel or bicycle basket, and off you go. And what a complete contrast to some of the articles and books I have read in recent years which turn the best sort of spontaneous picnic into a quasi-military operation requiring hours of shopping, preparation and cooking, not to mention all kinds of specialist containers and packaging.

Children know that the less time you spend getting ready, the more time you

will have to discover and enjoy beautiful spots covered in bluebells, primroses, violets, cowslips or celandines. Or lie on carpets of pine needles, bracken, heather or soft grass. Or lean against the trunk of a big, old oak tree. Or spread your blanket or mackintosh on a beach or a hillside or by the side of a stream. And eat.

And if, while you are eating your no-fuss, no-faff picnic, you listen very carefully, you will hear a chorus of voices in children's books all agreeing that food tastes so much better outside than it does indoors. So don't waste time with complicated dishes and salads and quiches, just take what you can and enjoy it while you can.

For more picnic treats see Swallows and Amazons Seed Cake (page 154); Very Nice Last Mouthful Cherry Cake (page 64); The Swallows' Squashed Fly Biscuits (page 162); Tinned Pineapple Cake (page 156); Great Fruit Cake (page 69); Diana's Favourite Fruity Fruit Cake (page 72); Attics and Apples (page 237); Mrs Banks' Bribery and Corruption Cocoanut Buns (page 54).

LASHINGS OF
HARD-BOILED EGGS

Hard-boiled eggs have a special status in the books of Enid Blyton. When she writes about them, she always manages to make them appear ultra-exciting and appealing rather than a boring and predictable element of teas and picnics. In fact, if I had to choose my favourite new treat after all the reading I conducted for this book, it would be hard-boiled eggs with a screw of salt.

Funnily enough, although I never come across any mention of the famous phrase 'lashings of ginger beer' which is so often attributed to Enid Blyton (not even in the Famous Five books which are awash with ginger pop), I did find a reference in *Five Go Down to the Sea* to "lashings of hard-boiled eggs". It was this that led me to consider this apparently very plain treat in a new light:

"The high tea that awaited them was truly magnificent. A huge ham…a salad fit for a king [including] lettuce, tomatoes, onions, radishes, mustard and cress carrots… and lashings of hard-boiled eggs."

No matter how delicious this eggy salad sounds, though, it's when hard-boiled eggs are eaten outside as part of a picnic lunch that they start to take on a new image. When *The Adventurous Four: Shipwrecked!* opens, the three siblings are running wild on the north-east coast of Scotland while Mother knits hard all day, until they meet up with a local boy and go off on sailing adventures fuelled by pineapple chunks, Nestle's milk, chocolate and hard-boiled eggs.

"It was a most peculiar breakfast, but the four children thought it was lovely. They had three loaves of bread with them, and some butter, and they dabbed the butter on to the chunks, took the eggs in their hand and bit first at the egg and then

171

at the bread. Jill put a paper of salt down on the deck for them to dip the eggs into."

The delight is in the detail of the 'paper of salt', a thoughtful and perfectly proportioned touch, like the little blue twists of salt you used to find in packets of plain crisps. In Enid Blyton's books, cooks and girls regularly pack a screw of salt (and sometimes pepper) to go with each egg, and I can't think of anything nicer than unpacking a picnic and finding these miniature makeshift cruets sitting neatly with the eggs.

2 large free-range eggs per person
Rock or sea salt

Sheet of greaseproof paper

1. Bring a large pan of water to the boil. Take it off the heat while you gently lower the eggs, one at a time, into the water. Put the pan back on the heat and simmer for 10 minutes.
2. Drain off the water and cover the eggs with cold water. Leave for a few minutes until cool enough to handle, then take the eggs out.
3. Rip the greaseproof paper into small (approximately 10 x 10 cm) squares. Place a square of paper in the palm of your hand and pour a little salt into the centre. Curl your fingers and bring up the paper so that you can twist it into a little screw that won't undo. Make a screw of salt per egg or per person. Greaseproof paper is good because it doesn't untwist, but you could also use newspaper. In fact, a crossword is the perfect size for a screw of salt, and useful entertainment after lashings of boiled eggs.

Dickon's Roasted Eggs

One of the joys of reading *The Secret Garden* is devouring the large number of tastebud-tingling descriptions of food eaten outdoors. Although it is fresh, plain and simple, it always sounds wonderful in this context. How about: "roasted eggs and potatoes and richly frothed new milk and oat-cakes and buns and heather honey and clotted cream".

All these food moments mean that, as sure as eggs is eggs, whenever I read *The Secret Garden* I have an urge to make roasted eggs. Although in Britain we have had roast beef, roast potatoes and roast chestnuts for centuries, and have recently embraced the more exotic roast peppers, figs and squash, somewhere along the way we lost the art of roasting eggs.

Roasted eggs have a very distinct appeal; it's as though the action of placing them in the glowing embers of a fire confers a certain hitherto-unknown cachet on the humble egg. And indeed they make the perfect outdoor food, cooking gently while children run around and play and work up an appetite.

In *The Secret Garden*, roasted eggs are a symbolic part of the diet that brings both Mary and Colin back to life and health. Dickon discovers "a deep little hollow where you could build a sort of tiny oven with stones and roast potatoes and eggs in it. Roasted eggs were a previously unknown luxury, and very hot potatoes with salt and fresh butter in them were fit for a woodland king – besides being deliciously satisfying."

Although you may wonder how it is that they don't crack or explode, I can assure you they do work.

1–2 EGGS PER PERSON

Baked potatoes, salt, butter and fresh milk, to serve

1. If you have a needle or something sharp to hand, make a tiny hole in the shell at one end of each egg.
2. Hold the egg under a tap or immerse it in water to wet the outside.
3. Place in the embers of a fire or in a cool (140°C/Gas Mark 2) oven.
4. Cook for an hour.
5. Leave to cool for a few minutes before peeling.
6. Serve with potatoes baked in the fire or oven, salt, butter and fresh milk.

WIND IN THE WILLOWS RIVER PICNIC CRESS SANDWIDGES

One hundred years after the publication of Kenneth Grahame's *The Wind in the Willows* the River Thames above Reading in Berkshire where the story takes place remains outstandingly beautiful, and is still one of the finest places for a river picnic from a "fat, wicker luncheon-basket" like the one Rat brings on his outing with Mole.

When Mole asks Rat what's inside, his reply is as crammed as the hamper:

"'There's cold chicken inside,' replied the Rat briefly; 'coldtonguecoldham-coldbeefpickledgherkinssaladfrenchrollscresssandwidgespottedmeatgingerbeer-lemonadesodawater —'

'O stop, stop,' cried the Mole in ecstasies: 'This is too much!'"

The Wind in the Willows reminds us that some treats never lose their charm over time; messing around in a boat, a full picnic hamper, a lovely stretch of river and all the time in the world to enjoy them. Yet we seem to have overlooked one, the cress

sandwidge [sic], and it would be a cruel loss to the joys of river picnics if we were to abandon it altogether. For the cress sandwidge is simplicity itself, and I would guess that everyone, young or old, sailor or landlubber, would enjoy one while sitting in a boat or on a checked wool blanket under a shady tree as time, and the river, go by.

Since we are talking about living life at a more leisurely pace, why not consider taking the time to grow your own cress to put in dainty sandwiches for a picnic? If you want cress for Saturday, sow some seeds on the Monday and within five days you'll be able to harvest your own spicy, peppery filling.

FIVE DAYS BEFORE THE PICNIC:
1 large plate
1 packet cress seeds
1 roll or pleat of cotton wool

1. Cover a large plate with a layer of cotton wool. Soak thoroughly with water, then pour off the excess.
2. Scatter the cress seeds over the surface of the cotton wool.
3. Leave in a bright, warm place (a kitchen windowsill is ideal). Do not allow the cotton wool to dry out. The cress is ready to eat when the leaves are fully formed.

ON THE DAY OF THE PICNIC:
Soft, salted butter   *Freshly harvested cress*
Thin slices of white or brown bread   *Salt (optional)*

1. Spread the butter thinly on the bread.
2. Cut the cress and scatter it thickly on half the slices. Add a sprinkling of salt, if desired.
3. Cover with the remaining slices, remove the crusts and cut the sandwiches into triangles.
4. Pack in a hamper and take the sandwiches to the river.

Ripe Plums and Summer Hols

Ripe plums appear throughout Enid Blyton's outdoor adventure stories like little, dark punctuation marks. In fact, like full stops, they appear with such regularity that as I reread the books I began to remember just how delicious a treat a handful of ripe plums can be, and to realise how often we, who should embrace one of the great British fruits, underestimate the joy of a ripe plum.

Ripe plums (they are never just 'plums') are a taste of the summer hols. Their season coincides perfectly with school-term dates, with the first plums ready to pick from mid-July and the last ones still ripening in late September. Ripe plums are ideal for picnics, perfect for eating outdoors on beaches, heather-covered hills or soft grass, up mountains, by streams, next to rivers, lakes and seas, preferably with a soft warm breeze and the sun on your face.

They are the epitome of fresh, seasonal, healthy, local, available food and yet we still manage to fill supermarket shelves with insipid, under-ripe, joyless plums. A good plum should be picked and eaten from the tree. It should be taut-skinned with a touch of tartness underneath, yet bursting with sweetness, warmth and juiciness. A handful or bagful of ripe plums can be picked, packed or pocketed in matter of minutes so that you can get on with enjoying the summer. And when you come to eat them (if you haven't gorged on them while picking) they are pleasingly easy and convenient, requiring no peeling, washing or preparation.

You have only to read classic English books by writers such as Enid Blyton, Arthur Ransome and E. Nesbit to be convinced that ripe plums are, pure and simple, a taste of summer, and that has to be one of the best treats of all.

SNUBBY'S' SUMMER
TOMATO SANDWICHES

"It's the sort of tea I like,' said Snubby, pleased. 'Potted meat and bread and butter, and tinned pineapple and cream, and cherry cake and biscuits, and our own tomato sandwiches and jam tarts.'"

If there is one sandwich that defines the teas and picnics in Enid Blyton's books, it is the tomato one. The popularity of this sandwich – always greeted with delight when the children unwrap their greaseproof paper parcels – intrigues me, because as a child I never encountered tomato sandwiches in real life. I'm not too sure I would have eaten them, anyway, because my earliest memories of tomatoes involve nastily cold, sour, squirty specimens with thick skins, green insides and no discernible tomato taste.

But now I realise that a good tomato sandwich, as enjoyed by children in the 1940s, could be a gastronomic delight. They would have been made with freshly picked, ripe, local tomatoes grown for taste rather than to meet supermarket levels of perfection and blandness, perhaps grown at home by their father or the gardener, or bought at the greengrocer's or market. These flavoursome tomatoes would be sliced thickly and sandwiched between two slices of good, white or wholemeal bread, preferably 'new' and 'home-made'. Most certainly the sandwiches would not have been made with flat, sliced, additive- and improver-laden white bread that goes soggy instantly on contact with tomatoes, for part of the joy of a good tomato sandwich is the bread, which soaks up all the lovely juices.

It amuses me that these days we are happy to eat Italian bruschetta or French baguettes with tomato salad, and yet we overlook the delights of the humble,

English tomato sandwich. So here is my recipe for a sandwich to be wrapped in greaseproof paper, packed in a satchel with a bottle of cool lemonade, and eaten outdoors.

For good bread, see Awfully Good New-Made Bread (page 27).

SERVES 1

Wholemeal or good-quality white bread
1–2 large ripe, red, juicy, tasty tomatoes, at room temperature
Sea salt

1. Slice the bread into reasonably thick slices.
2. Slice the tomatoes, not too thinly.
3. Arrange the tomatoes on a slice of bread so that the surface is covered.
4. Sprinkle with salt and cover with a second slice of bread.
5. Cut in two, wrap in paper or foil, pack with a bottle of lemonade, a Famous Five story, map, compass, binoculars, swimming costume and towel, and off you go.

VARIATIONS
- Sourdough bread has a particular affinity with tomatoes and makes a wonderful open sandwich – not practical for picnics, but worth trying at home.
- If you don't want the bread to soak up all the juice too quickly, you can butter it before adding the tomatoes.
- Ground black pepper on the tomatoes adds a little extra bite.
- A drizzle of extra virgin olive oil, a few basil leaves, or a squeeze of lemon are all acceptable, if not terribly authentic, additions.

SEVEN LITTLE AUSTRALIANS' DAMPER

"If you imagine you are going to read of model children, with perhaps a naughtily-inclined one to point a moral, you had better lay down the book immediately... Not one of the seven is really good, for the very excellent reason that Australian children never are."

With these direct and challenging introductory words of warning, Ethel Turner sets the scene for a refreshingly different nineteenth-century story, and one which confirms that the best Australian books for children all over the world are those with a uniquely Australian flavour.

Although many of the elements of *Seven Little Australians*, first published in 1894, are standard in contemporary novels – the large, mischievous family, the bright, wayward heroine, the stern, uncomprehending father and the flighty young stepmother – there are enough differences in culture, location and attitude to make this a truly Australian classic. Children from respectable families in British and American novels are never quite as thrillingly messy or dirty, nor do they knowingly call their house 'Misrule', or boldy address their stepmother by her first name, or have the adventure of visiting a sheep station three hundred miles from Sydney.

Nor would they ever have a picnic in a very "out-of-the-way" spot in the already out-of-the-way bush. At this point, non-Australian readers may feel they are on firmer ground; despite the fact that the children are surround by tall blue and red gums, kangaroos and bell-birds, rifle-birds and coach-whips, the seven young Woolcots eat food their British contemporaries would recognise: roast fowl, apple tarts, fruit salad and apricot turnovers.

That is, until Ethel Turner reminds us forcefully where we are when Mr Gillet, the stockman, makes a damper "by special request" for afternoon tea:

"Mr Giller merely tossed some flour from a bag out upon a plate, added a pinch of salt and some water; then he slapped it into a cake of dough, and laid it on the ashes of the fire, covering it all over with the hot, silver ash.

'*How* dirty!' said Nell, elevating her pretty little nose.

But when it was cooked, and Mr Gillet lifted it up and dusted the ash away – lo! it was high and light and beautifully white.

So they ate it, and took mental marginal notes to make it in the paddocks at Misrule for each and every picnic to come."

Really, there is nothing to beat a good, fresh damper. With its simple philosophy, ingredients, preparation and cooking method, it encapsulates the essence of the Australian makeshift camp-fire experience. I know because I have eaten damper still hot from a small baking pot after a long, long day's work in a winery in the Barossa Valley, and it would take a lot to beat this honest treat. It tastes of the bush, the outback, the outdoors, and it's what roots the Seven Little Australians firmly in their homeland.

And as for what happens after the picnic – well, that would be telling. Trust me, it's quite some ending.

A damper is an ultra-simple bread that is is cooked in the coals of a fire. It was developed by stockmen, who carried only the most basic of rations to sustain them and therefore had to make their own bread from scratch. The ingredients were flour, water, salt and sometimes milk and baking soda. A real damper is cooked in the ashes of a camp fire: the ashes are flattened and the dough is placed on them for ten minutes, then covered in ashes and cooked until done. It can also be cooked in a hole, about 25 cm deep, that is filled with hot coals and ash, in a camp or Dutch oven, or in a kitchen oven.

Although there are all kinds of variations on the damper theme these days, I'm giving a very basic recipe, similar to the one in *Seven Little Australians* that inspires the children to take note of this surprising treat.

MAKES 1 MEDIUM LOAF

300 g (approx.) self-raising flour

1 generous teaspoon salt

1 teaspoon sugar

250 ml (approx.) liquid (I use half water and half milk)

Tea, Vegemite, butter, cheese, jam or golden syprup, to serve

Baking tray, lightly oiled, if you are using a conventional oven

1. Preheat the oven to 180°C/Gas Mark 6. Alternatively, cook your damper on a camp fire.
2. Place the flour, salt and sugar in a mixing bowl. Make a well in the centre, and, working quickly, pour in sufficient liquid (about 200 ml) to bring the ingredients together with your hand and make a firm, sticky dough that is not too dry. Add more liquid if necessary.
3. Shape the dough into a round, flattish, round loaf. Cut a cross on top with a sharp knife.
4. Oven: Place the dough on the baking tray and bake for 40 minutes or until the damper is golden brown on top and sounds hollow when tapped on the base.
5. Camp fire: Flatten the ashes, place the damper on them, and leave for 10 minutes, then cover the surface of the damper with ashes. Leave for 25–30 minutes until the bread sounds hollow when tapped on the base.
6. Serve with tea, Vegemite, butter, cheese, jam or golden syrup

JEREMY AND JEMIMA'S MORE-JAM-THAN-PUFF JAM PUFFS

At first glance it's difficult to believe that the whimsical, light-hearted and affectionate *Chitty Chitty Bang Bang* was written by the same man who created the often cruel, dark and sadistic world of James Bond. The two seem poles apart, until you realise that food, fizzy drinks and cars feature strongly in both, although I suspect James Bond never knew the delights of a clapped-out old car, and he certainly never packed hampers full of jam puffs to enjoy with his Pommery '50.

Ian Fleming relished writing descriptions of food (he once wrote, 'My contri-bution to thriller-writing has been to attempt the total stimulation of the reader all the way through, even to his taste buds') and *Chitty Chitty Bang Bang* is an epicurean delight. Only someone who loved food could pack an imaginary hamper for a day's outing with "hard-boiled eggs, cold sausages, bread-and-butter sandwiches, jam puffs (with, of course, like all good jam puffs, more jam than puff) and bottles and bottles of the best fizzy lemonade and orange squash".

Wouldn't it be marvellous to re-enact the story and cross the Channel from Kent to France in a flying car, land on a warm beach to swim and clamber on the rocks, then settle down to enjoy "every single hard-boiled egg, every single cold sausage, and every single strawberry jam puff" before becoming embroiled in a French adventure and being rewarded with the closely guarded recipe for 'Monsieur Bon-Bon's Secret Fooj'?

185

Much as I like the sound of 'Fooj' (the French way of saying 'fudge' according to Fleming) and am grateful for the recipe provided in the book, I found that what I really wanted to make were the more-jam-than-puff jam puffs that Jeremy and Jemima enjoy as part of their beach picnic. Then I can live in hope that while I am eating them James Bond will emerge from the Channel wearing nothing more than his swimming trunks.

Jam puffs can be made in two ways: in individual portions or as one large puff which is then sliced. With the aim of having the maximum jam : puff ratio, I am giving a recipe for one, large jam-packed puff. But it will also work if you prefer to make a dozen small enclosed puffs, as long as you remember to reduce the cooking time accordingly.

MAKES 1 LARGE JAM PUFF (SERVES 12)
1 x 475 g packet puff pastry (preferably containing 2 ready-rolled sheets)
1 jar jam (whatever flavour you prefer)
Milk or water, for sealing
1 egg white, lightly beaten
Caster sugar, for sprinkling
Whipped cream, to serve (optional)

Baking tray lined with baking parchment

1. Preheat the oven to 200°C/Gas Mark 6.
2. If you are using ready-rolled pastry, place one sheet on the baking tray. If not, roll out the pastry into a large rectangle about 5 mm thick. Cut into two equal pieces and place one on the baking tray.
3. Spread the sheet of pastry with a thick layer of jam to within 1 cm of the edge. Lightly wet the edges with water or milk.

4. Cover with the second sheet of pastry and press the edges together to seal, turning them upwards slightly to prevent the jam escaping during cooking.

5. Bake in the oven for 20 minutes, then remove and brush the surface with the egg white. Sprinkle with the caster sugar, and return to the oven for a further 10 minutes until the pastry is golden brown.

6. Transfer the tray to a wire rack and leave the jam puff to cool. When cool, slice the puff into strips, without pressing too hard, and arrange on a plate or pack in a hamper. Jam puffs are also delicious served with whipped cream.

Gerald's Picnic Goosegogs

I have always had a soft spot for the underrated and all-too-often overlooked gooseberry, and feel we should appreciate this humble, hardy, hard-working fruit more than we do at the moment. Although it's the stuff of baby jokes and a tag for lonesome, superfluous singletons, the easy-to-grow gooseberry with its distinctive flavour is a wonderfully versatile fruit that makes excellent fools, tarts, crumbles, ices, jams and sauces. And, as Gerald in The Enchanted Castle *reminds us, "goosegogs" are also delicious on their own, eaten outside in summer from a recycled box, as part of a picnic tea on a fine grass carpet.*

"It was a generous tea. A long loaf, butter in a cabbage-leaf, a bottle of milk, cake, and large, smooth, yellow gooseberries in a box that had once held an extra-sized bottle of somebody's matchless something for the hair and moustache… there was a happy, hungry silence, broken only by those brief, impassioned suggestions natural to such an occasion:

'More cake, please.'

'Milk ahoy, there.'

'Chuck us the goosegogs.'"

At last Gerald is full, and declares, "'Well, I'm a new man, but I couldn't eat so much as another goosegog if you paid me.'"

Here's a boy who knows his gooseberries. Most people think of them as green, hard, hairy and sour when in fact there are all sorts of gooseberries in a range of colours from pale yellow through shades of green to pinkish-red to light maroon, with or without hair, small, medium or large. Small, green ones picked in early summer are the ones to cook with, but the late-ripening, thin-skinned gooseberries are the ones to eat straight from the bush or box. Today, just as in the time of Gerald and the Edwardians, the pale yellow, translucent, large dessert 'Leveller' gooseberry is regarded as the ultimate eating variety.

So next time you are planning a picnic, why not do as Gerald does and look for a punnet of sweet gooseberries (or pick your own) and enjoy the revival of a quintessentially English summer fruit.

And, should you need any more persuading, there is nothing like being on familiar terms with a fruit whose name has been affectionately corrupted to the funny and endearing 'goosegog'.

EASY-PEASY
LEMON-SQUEEZY LEMONADE

O ceans of lemonade are drunk by children in fiction. Thousands of mouth-watering references are made to its delicious, zesty, refreshing qualities. It is taken on picnics, chilled in streams, enjoyed in sunny gardens, packed in hampers, stowed in bicycle baskets, opened at birthday parties, bought in village stores, knocked back in cafés and tea shops, stashed away in tree houses, tents, caravans, caves and boats. It is a universal indicator of the happy moments of childhood, of days full of fresh air and freedom. And although some of the lemonade is the bottled, carbonated variety, it is the fresh home-made version that is the quintessen-tial lemonade of summer in children's literature.

When my children were little they would have said making lemonade was 'pips'. In other words, easy, as in 'easy peasy lemon squeezy'. And so it is. But it would be even easier if we had magic trees growing within arm's reach, like the one in *The Folk of the Faraway Tree* by Enid Blyton which produces lemons just as the children want to make lemonade:

"There was as much lemonade as anyone liked, because, in a most friendly manner, the Faraway Tree suddenly began to grow ripe yellow lemons on the branches round about. All Moon-Face had to do was pick them, cut them in half, and squeeze them into a jug. Then he added sugar and water, and the children drank the lemonade!"

There are several ways to make lemonade. One is the method described in the extract above and this is the basis for the first recipe, which makes fresh, zesty lemonade.

FRESH, READY-TO-DRINK LEMONADE

Makes approx. 1 litre

6 large lemons (unwaxed)

2–4 tablespoons caster sugar

Ice and lemon slices, to serve

1. Cut the lemons in half and squeeze them on a lemon squeezer so that the pips don't go into the juice. Pour the juice into a jug. A little pulp in the lemonade won't do any harm and will add to the flavour.
2. Add 2 tablespoons of the sugar and stir well to dissolve.
3. Add 1 litre water, taste and adjust the sugar level as necessary. Some people like their lemonade very tart and others like it sweet.
4. Store in the fridge if not serving imediately.
5. When ready to serve, add plenty of ice and a few slices of lemon, and stir.

HOLIDAY LEMONADE

The second recipe is for lemonade that takes advantage of the lazier pace of summer holidays. It is made a day in advance and is wonderfully tasty and full-flavoured as a result. I first tasted lemonade made this way while sitting in the sun on a hot summer's day with my friend, Caroline. I remembered the moment and the delicious lemonade when I came to write this book, and Caroline has very kindly given me her recipe. By coincidence, it is known in her family as 'Holiday Lemon-ade', and is made in huge quantities at the family home in Portugal, with lemons picked from the trees in Grandpa's field.

Makes approx. 1 litre
6–7 lemons (unwaxed)
6–7 dessertspoons sugar
6–7 tea cups boiling water
Ice, to serve

1. Squeeze the lemons into a large jug – pips, pulp and all.
2. Add the grated zest or strips of zest from 2–3 lemons.
3. Stir in the sugar.
4. Pour on the boiling water and stir well.
5. Cover and leave in the fridge overnight if possible, but at least until cool; then strain and keep well chilled.
6. Serve with ice.

GORGEOUS GINGER BEER

I would hazard a guess that no one in children's literature drinks as much ginger beer as the Famous Five. It's true that plenty of other characters enjoy the odd swig or two, but Julian, Dick, Anne and George seem to positively exist on it. Julian explains the attraction in *Five Run Away Together*: "'I must say ginger-beer is a gorgeous drink – it seems to go with simply everything.'" And they regularly put that statement to the test – ginger beer with tinned sardines, anyone?

But I have yet to come across any description of 'lashings' of ginger beer (the Famous Five only ever have lashings of hard-boiled eggs – not quite the same) so I have to assume that this phrase was coined by someone else, and not by Enid Blyton herself. But never mind. I don't think we should let this minor disappointment detract from our vicarious, nostalgic enjoyment of the quintessential picnic-followed-by-adventure beverage, with its suggestions of summer holidays, fresh air, freedom and exploding bottles.

Ginger beer is great fun to make, and very easy. You can use a kit if you like (available on the internet) or adopt the approach of which the Famous Five would approve, and have a go at making it yourself.

Plan to make it three days before your picnic. If you use plastic mineral-water bottles you will avoid the danger of glass bottles exploding as the pressure builds up inside. As you need two 1.5 litre plastic bottles you could plan to use most of the water for the ginger beer (this also saves having to wash and rinse used bottles). The ginger beer can then be transported in the plastic bottles.

The recipe can be adapted to suit your taste by adding more or less ginger and sugar.

Note: Ginger beer made by this method is not guaranteed to be 100 per cent alcohol-free. It may contain a tiny amount of alcohol.

MAKES APPROX. 2.5 LITRES
1 lemon, skin and pith removed, thinly sliced
150 caster sugar (more if you want a sweeter drink)
20–30 g fresh grated ginger (microplane graters are excellent for this)
2 teaspoons cream of tartar
2.5 litres boiling water
5 g dried yeast or ordinary baking yeast
Ice, to serve

2 1.5 litre plastic bottles (see above)

1. Place the lemon slices, sugar, ginger to taste and cream of tartar in a large, non-metallic bowl. Pour over the boiling water and leave to cool until lukewarm.
2. Stir in the yeast. Cover with a tea towel and leave in a warm place for 24 hours.
3. Now skim off any yeast from the surface and strain the liquid into a large jug through muslin or a fine nylon sieve; take care to leave any sediment in the bowl.
4. Using a funnel, pour the strained liquid into the clean bottles. Make sure you don't fill the bottles to the top but leave at least a 10-cm gap to allow for a build-up of gas.
5. Screw the bottle tops on tightly and leave in a cool place. Check the bottles from time to time, and partly unscrew the tops to release some gas. When the ginger is fizzy it's ready to drink; this will take 12–36 hours.
6. Drink when fresh – home-made ginger beer goes stale very quickly.
7. Serve with lashings of ice and fun.

GOING
OUT

It may seem a little perverse to include recipes for fictional treats that are purchased in shops or enjoyed in cafés and tea rooms. Why would anyone want to bother making these at home when they can be obtained so much more easily over a counter?

Well, the answer is that although the treats in this section are all bought they are either no longer around today or, if they can be found, they taste immeasurably better when made at home. It's worth remembering that when the majority of the books I cover were written, there were no nationwide supermarket chains or huge

food manufacturers to supply identikit products to every outlet. So the cakes, pastries and ices featured in stories up to the 1960s are usually made on a small scale by just one person on the premises of a shop or café, in what was just a larger version of a domestic kitchen, which gives them an appealingly home-made character.

And really, no éclair you can buy nowadays can compare to a fresh, home-made, cream-filled one, no matter how posh the packaging. And how else will you discover why raspberry cakes make Mary Poppins cry 'Strike me pink!' – because you certainly won't find the answer in a supermarket. And as for coconut kisses, every child should try making William Brown's favourite sweetmeat once, instead of heading for the pick 'n' mix counter.

Going out has become the new staying in. Children are so used to being taken out for meals and treats that the idea of buying treats is now widely accepted; indeed, for many children it is the norm. And this trend is reflected in childrens' fiction. Contemporary characters eat out, buy in, have food delivered, run round to the shops for a treat, and fill their supermarket trolley with baked goods. But it does no harm, once in a while, to revisit the past and take something good from it. So why not make something sweet and delicious instead of buying it?

For more treats that are bought by children in stories see: Fresh and Gooey Macaroons (page 44); Sara's Warming Currant Buns (page 226); Milly-Molly-Mandy's Muffin Man Muffins (page 56).

MARY POPPINS' STRIKE-ME-PINK RASPBERRY JAM CAKES

When it comes to the printed page versus the animated screen, I am of the persuasion that an original book is always better than a derivative film. I'm not saying there aren't some wonderful films based on children's classics; it's just that nothing can ever, ever beat the pictures and images and tastes you create in your own imagination when you're engrossed in a wonderful book.

Mary Poppins is a fine example of the slippage between book and film. Some adults are shocked when they encounter the vain, acerbic and often bad-tempered literary Mary Poppins for the first time, for she is far removed from the magical, appealing, sweet-voiced Julie Andrews. And she has a much larger appetite.

In *Mary Poppins* she and Bert jump into an idyllic chalk pavement scene he has created, and are whisked away to "a little open space filled with sunlight,"

"And there on a green table was Afternoon Tea!

A pile of raspberry jam cakes as high as Mary Poppins' waist stood in the centre, and beside it tea was boiling in a big brass urn. Best of all, there were two plates of whelks and two pins to pick them out with.

'Strike me pink!' said Mary Poppins. That was what she said when she was pleased."

In a delightfully extravagant and markedly un-Poppinish manner (to those who still think of her as the film version), she and Bert proceed to work their way through the whelks, drink three cups of tea and eat the entire heap of cakes together.

Raspberry jam cakes sound delicious, don't they? And yet, even though I had never in reality eaten any like the ones Mary Poppins enjoys, I *had* in my imagination. They came on a doily on a proper cake plate, and were dusted with icing sugar. They were small enough to be eaten in two or three dainty bites, and in large quantities. They were pale yellow, sweet, softly spongy with a contrasting fresh, acidic burst of raspberry in the centre. They were not too sticky (Mary Poppins does not get sticky after eating sweet cakes) and they were not too filling. And they always elicited cries of "Strike me pink!"

These raspberry cakes sounded so good to me that I had to make some. I searched and searched for a recipe after and eventually I found one in an old cooking booklet that belonged to my mother-in-law, and I have brought this up to date.

MAKES 12 CAKES

225 g self-raising flour

1 teaspoon baking powder

85 g caster sugar, plus extra for
  sprinkling

85 g butter

1 large egg, beaten

2–3 tablespoons milk, plus extra for
  brushing

6 teaspoons raspberry jam

Tea, to serve

Baking tray, greased with butter or lined with baking parchment

1. Preheat the oven to 180°C/Gas Mark 4.
2. Sift the flour and baking powder into a large bowl. Stir in the sugar. Rub in the butter until the mixture resembles fine breadcrumbs.
3. Add the beaten egg and enough milk to make a soft dough. On a lightly floured work surface, shape into a flattish rectangle and divide into roughly equal pieces with a knife. Roll each piece into a ball.
3. Flatten each ball slightly, then make a little depression in the centre and bring the edges up, as if you were making a very basic clay pot. Place ½ teaspoon of the raspberry jam in the middle of each cake.
4. With your fingers, gently bring the edges together to close the dough over the jam. Then turn the cakes over and place them well apart on the baking tray.
5. Brush the tops with milk and sprinkle each cake with a little caster sugar.
6. Bake in the oven for 15–20 minutes until the cakes are pale gold, but not brown. Do not overcook them, as you want to keep them relatively moist. If you cook them too long they become biscuity.
7. Transfer the tray to a wire rack and leave the cakes to cool.
8. Pile them on a plate and serve with tea.

Mrs Corry's
Gilt Gingerbread

Hansel and Gretel is one of my favourite fairy tales. Although I've always thought the children are a little naïve about the witch, I love the descriptions and illustrations of the edible gingerbread house. So I think the chapter in *Mary Poppins* in which the Banks children are taken by Mary Poppins to buy gingerbread from a decidedly witchy old lady is a brilliant variation on the Hansel and Gretel theme, and I reckon the film-makers missed out on a great junior Hammer House of Horrors effect when they decided to omit this scene.

The tiny Mrs Corry sells gingerbread in a strange, shabby little shop:

"Inside the shop they could dimly see the glass-topped counter that ran round three sides of it. And in a case under the glass were rows and rows of dark, dry gingerbread, each slab so studded with gilt stars that the shop itself seemed to be faintly lit by them."

Mrs Corry keeps her two huge, sad, round-faced daughters imprisoned but flatters visiting children and, instead of eating them, she lets them eat *her*. In a macabre and cannibalistic inversion of the traditional story in which Hansel offers a chicken bone instead of his finger as proof that he is not fat enough to be eaten, Mrs Corry breaks off her barley sugar fingers and gives them to the twins, John and Barbara. And although she treats her own offspring appallingly, she is disconcertingly generous to Jane and Michael when they buy the "delicious dark cakes".

Mrs Corry's gingerbread is a version of the traditional gilt gingerbread that was sold at the great fairs of England for centuries, which did indeed have gold leaf (or the cheaper 'Dutch gilt') on top to make it look more attractive and luxurious. In a truly magical postscript to the shopping expedition, Jane and Michael save their gilt stars and put them for safe keeping in their bedroom drawers. But later that night Mary Poppins, Mrs Corry and her enormous daughters creep into the children's room, take the stars and glue them on to the dark night sky.

So this recipe for gilt gingerbread includes gold stars. You can cut your own out of gold card or use the ready-made ones available from stationers. Just make sure they are not swallowed, because Mary Poppins may not be on hand with a spoonful of sugar to help them go down.

MAKES 12 GINGERBREAD SQUARES

125 g butter

1 tablespoon black treacle

1 tablespoon golden syrup

100 g dark soft brown sugar

225 g self-raising flour

2 teaspoons ground ginger

½ teaspoon mixed spice

¼ teaspoon grated nutmeg

½ teaspoon bicarbonate of soda

4 tablespoons milk

2 eggs, lightly beaten

150 g (approx.) icing sugar

1–2 lemons

12 gold stars (or gold or yellow sweets)

Square (22 x 22 cm) cake tin, greased with butter and lined with baking parchment

1. Preheat the oven to 160°C/Gas Mark 3.
2. Melt the butter with the treacle, golden syrup and sugar in a large pan over a low heat. Leave to cool slightly.
3. Sift the flour and spices into a large mixing bowl.
4. Dissolve the bicarbonate of soda in the milk and add this and the contents of the pan to the bowl.
5. Mix together well, then spoon into the cake tin.
6. Bake for 25–30 minutes until a metal skewer or sharp knife inserted in the

gingerbread comes out clean. Take care not to overcook.

7. Leave the gingerbread in its tin on a wire rack to cool for 5 minutes, then turn out and leave to cool completely.

8. When the gingerbread is completely cold, make the icing. Sift the icing sugar into a bowl, add the juice of one of the lemons and mix well until you have thick, spreadable icing. Add more juice or icing sugar if necessary. Spread the icing over the top of the gingerbread.

9. Decorate with the stars or sweets and cut into twelve squares. The gingerbread is best eaten fresh.

ST CLARE'S ÉCLAIRS

A lthough it doesn't happen too often (many young readers' books are set in more austere times than ours) children sometimes go out to a tea shop for a special treat. Fatty, the gourmet in Enid Blyton's Five Find-Outer books, is a great connoisseur of tea shops and thinks nothing of spending his cash on wonderfully lavish teas, cakes and ices, while in many school stories the girls and boys frequently fill themselves with good food in the local tea shop (and there is *always* one nearby).

But surely the ultimate in tea-shop treat excitement is to be taken out by a favourite schoolteacher? In *The O'Sullivan Twins*, the history teacher, Miss Lewis (a good sort) takes the first form to the theatre and then for a marvellous tea:

"'Buns and jam! Fruit cake! Meringues! Chocolate éclairs!'... Golly, it was a spread!"

The éclair is often seen as the height of sophistication, a genteel fancy to be enjoyed in a tea room where there are waitresses and plenty of snow-white table linen. Its Frenchness makes it sound even more chic, so it's amusing that the girls are so heartily English in their delight, and show no Gallic restraint when it comes to tucking in.

The éclair also has a reputation for being difficult to make in a domestic kitchen, which is probably why it became such tea-shop or patisserie speciality. But this needn't be the case. There is nothing to beat a fresh, billowing home-made éclair filled with sweet whipped cream and drizzled with dark bitter chocolate, and choux pastry is amazingly simple to prepare. Chocolate éclairs have been Alice's pièce de résistance since she learnt to make them at a children's cookery course a few years ago. They are *that* easy to make.

MAKES 16–18 ÉCLAIRS

150 g plain flour

Pinch of salt

120 g butter

4 eggs

FOR THE FILLING:

1 x 284 ml carton or 300 ml double or
*   whipping cream*

50 g icing sugar

120 g dark chocolate, melted

Large baking tray, lined with a Teflon sheet or baking parchment

1. Preheat the oven to 200°C/Gas Mark 6.
2. Sift the flour and salt into a bowl.
3. Place the butter in a large pan with 250 ml water and place over a medium heat until the butter has melted and the mixture begins to bubble.

4. Remove the pan from the heat and immediately add all the flour. Beat vigorously with a wooden spoon or electric whisk until there are no lumps and the mixture comes away from the sides of the pan.

5. Gradually add the eggs one at a time, beating in well. The mixture should now look smooth and glossy.

6. Spoon or pipe small circles or lengths of pastry on to the baking tray, leaving a space between each.

7. Bake for 20–25 minutes or until golden brown.

8. Transfer the tray to a wire rack, leave the éclairs to cool for a few minutes then pierce the side of each éclair with a sharp knife in order to let the steam escape.

9. It is best to fill the éclairs just before serving to prevent them going soggy. Whip the cream with the icing sugar until soft peaks are formed. Split each éclair horizontally with a sharp knife and place a spoonful of sweetened cream inside. When all the éclairs have been filled, drizzle or spread the melted chocolate over their tops.

Sweet Memories

I don't embrace nostalgia purely for the sake of it, but I do think there are certain, old-fashioned things that are worth preserving. And the traditional sweet shop is definitely one of them. Going to a sweet-filled emporium, clutching your pocket money, and spending as much time as you like deliberating over and collating your purchases, is so much more fun than picking up a plastic bag of a single variety of sweet and taking it to the cash desk of a large, anonymous shop or supermarket.

So I am delighted that we are seeing the renaissance of the old-time sweet shop selling all the old favourites, which are weighed and bagged and handed over to the purchaser. It's good to know that new generations of sweet-eaters can experience the delight of the independent sweet shop as well as reading about it in books such as Linnets and Valerians *by* Elizabeth Goudge. *This is the scene when the children visit Emma Cobley's sweet shop for the first time:*

"After a heated discussion, which lasted a full ten minutes, they chose a pennyworth of peppermint lumps that looked like striped brown bees, a pennyworth of lemon sweets the colour of pale honey, a penny-ha'penny-worth of satin pralines in colours of pink and mauve, and a pennyworth of liquorice allsorts. And out of pure goodness of heart Emma Cobley added for nothing a packet of sherbet. They did not know what that was, and she had to show them how to put a pinch of powder on their tongues and then stand with their tongues out enjoying the glorious refreshing fizz."

They leave the shop sucking the pralines: "they were crisp and crackling on the outside and soft and squishy inside. The moment when the teeth crashed through from the outside was sheer heaven."

What a lovely, evocative description; it takes real knowledge to write with such epicurean delight. The satin praline was one of the stars of the Edwardian sweet tray and a favourite of Elizabeth Goudge (born 1900), and it is being revived by specialist sweet shops together with many other classic sweets that were in danger of extinction. We may not call it a satin praline these days – it is now a 'chocolate satin' – but I am delighted to say that you can still buy this and many other delicacies such as bullseyes, humbugs, acid drops, barley sugar and pineapple chunks. It's good to know that sweet memories are still available on the high street.

For real sweets, I recommend the www.aquarterof.co.uk website and the Sugar Boy shops and website www.sugarboy.co.uk. Also, if you do a little local research, you will probably find that there is a traditional sweet shop near you, for they are reappearing everywhere.

JUST COCONUT KISSES

"In the matter of sweets, William frankly upheld the superiority of quantity over quality."

Richmal Crompton's William inhabits a world of pea-shooters, popguns, catapults, air guns, comics, fabulously imaginative games, lawless gangs of boys swarming in sweet shops, aniseed balls, bullseyes, pear drops, pineapple crisps, cokernut kisses [sic], acid-drop fights, liquorice sticks as 'peace offerings', and fluffy toffee in trouser pockets. Some of the details may have changed (these days, boys' pockets are more likely to contain branded sweets than ones with evocative names, and perhaps fewer lethal weapons) but Richmal Crompton is spot-on when it comes to knowing just what is and isn't important to an eleven-year-old boy.

Above all, she understands that sweets are central to boys' lives. Indeed, 'William Goes to the Pictures', the opening story in the very first William book, is under-pinned by 12 ounces of gooseberry eyes, which are meted out at every twist and turn of the brilliantly funny narrative and are the perfect accompaniment to his day of wide-eyed wonder and bewilderment at the antics of the adult world.

Making these "emerald green dainties" would be very tricky, so I'm giving a recipe for the other shop-bought treat which, for me, stands out in the list of William's favourite sweet treats: the cokernut kiss.

This is the delicacy William discovers for the first time in a subsequent story when "the ideal of his childhood – perhaps of everyone's childhood – was realised" and he is left in charge of a sweet shop with predictably entertaining results. "He had a sweet shop... It was all his – all these rows and rows of gleaming bottles of sweets... those boxes and boxes... of chocolate" and as he surveys his new kingdom, his eyes light up at the sight of the box of cokernut kisses. However, he soon realises this treat has a slight downside:

"Its only drawback was its instability. It melted away in the mouth at once. So much so that almost before William was aware of it he was confronted by the empty box. He returned to the more solid charms of the Pineapple Crisp."

Coconut kisses are an old favourite and are very simple to make. They are a cheat's version of coconut macaroons; sweet and chewy, and like little kisses of coconut on the lips.

MAKES 40 (sufficient to test William's preference for quantity rather than quality)
1 x 500 g tin condensed milk
250–300 g shredded coconut
1 dessertspoon vanilla extract
1 egg white

Baking tray lined with baking parchment

1. Preheat the oven to 140°C/Gas Mark 2.
2. In a mixing bowl, combine the condensed milk with 250 g of the coconut, and the vanilla extract, until well mixed and firm.
3. Whisk the egg white and stir it into the mixture until it is stiff enough to hold its shape. Add more coconut if necessary.
4. With a teaspoon, put small, rough heaps of the mixture on the tray; leave enough room for each heap to spread slightly during cooking.
5. Bake for 8–10 minutes until slightly browned and firm.
6. Transfer the tray to a wire rack and leave the coconut kisses to cool on a windowsill at optimum height for light-fingered boys.

REAL DAIRY ICES

Although they never actually refer to their favourite haunt as such, Enid Blyton's Five Find-Outers are the original English milk-bar kids. They are urban children who roam around fictional Peterswood (located close to the very real Marlow and Burnham Beeches in Buckinghamshire) where there is a high street, a railway station, a local policeman, Mr Goon, and any number of cafés, sweet shops, coffee shops and lemonade shops where they can spend Fatty's money on treats, watch the world go by and pick up the best gossip, clues and leads.

Their signature treat is "real" ice cream (or "ices" as they often call them, which somehow adds an extra frisson of coldness) bought and eaten at the dairy which is their equivalent of a milk bar. The Find-Outers eat up to four ices a day in the summer holidays; they spend most of their off-duty time working out how to pay for the next round, and when a mystery has been solved they celebrate with double-size specials.

No matter how often it's consumed, Enid Blyton always manages to capture the wonderful coolness of ice cream, the delight of letting it slip slowly down the throat while the rest of the world boils in the sun. There is never any mention of flavours for this is pure, simple, basic ice cream made with milk, the kind that has little shards of crystals embedded in its softness and leaves a clean, refreshing aftertaste.

We rarely come across freshly made milk ice cream these days (it must be eaten fresh because the frozen milk content goes sour quite quickly) as we no longer have milk bars or dairies with café arrangements, and it's rare to find ultra-plain ices on sale. But a milk ice is utterly delicious and palate-cleansing, a cross between an ice cream and a sorbet, and is a treat worth reviving, best made early on a hot summer's day as something to look forward to when the temperature rises.

The number of egg yolks required for this recipe makes it a good partner for Cook's Immensely Enjoyable Meringues (see page 233) which require egg whites. Alternatively, freeze the egg whites two at a time in polythene bags.

Milk ice cream can be made without an ice-cream maker, but you will need a suitable container such as a Pyrex bowl or plastic food container/tub/sandwich box.

Serves 4–6
8 egg yolks
150 g caster sugar
750 ml full-cream milk

1. Whisk the eggs and sugar in a bowl until pale, thick and creamy.
2. In large pan gently warm the milk to blood heat (do not boil) then pour it over the eggs and sugar. Mix well.
3. Pour the liquid back into pan and place on a low heat. Stir constantly until the mixture thickens – this will only take a few minutes and it will not be very thick – then remove from the heat and leave to cool.
4. When cool, pour into an ice-cream maker and follow the manufacturer's instructions. Alternatively, pour the liquid into a plastic container and place in the freezer until solid. Remove from time to time and stir well, mixing in any ice crystals that form around the edge and on the ssurface.
5. Remove the ice from the freezer about 15 minutes before serving.

POSH ICE CREAM SUNDAE

*T*he *Family from One End Street* was one of my favourite books as a child, and I read it avidly and in all innocence. I didn't know that in some quarters it was considered unsuitable reading for children due to the 'working class' nature of the family, nor was I aware that the author had also been accused of being patronising. I simply loved the scrapes the children get into, the wonderful things that turn up at the right moments, and the very amusing way in which Eve Garnett gently exposes the pretensions of those who consider themselves a cut above the Ruggles.

The Ruggles are a plain, bread-and-butter, fish-and-chips, tea-and-buns type of family with no airs and graces. They are not posh and they don't eat posh food such as biscuits of the very best 'selected' brands, sandwiches that are "marvels of crustless refinement", or pale pink and green cakes with "a look of great breeding". And they call an ice cream an ice cream, not a sundae.

In fact, they don't even know what a sundae is until they are taken to "one of Lyons's largest and most 'Posh' tea shops" for a "Regular Blow Out". When their host orders a sundae they are reassured "to hear it was only a very superior kind of ice cream" – or, you could say, an ice cream out in its Sunday best. Because it's amazing what a sundae glass, a long spoon, some sauce, a few wafers, a maraschino cherry, a blob of whipped cream and a live orchestra in the background can do to the humble ice cream.

Sundaes make a lovely treat for a special meal or birthday or celebration and, much as I love sparkly bits and paper parasols, I do think the simplest ones are the best. So the sundaes I make comprise just a couple of scoops of very good vanilla ice cream served in a tall glass with the best-tasting, home-made warm chocolate sauce and perhaps a swirl of whipped cream and a few fresh raspberries or strawberries.

POSH CHOCOLATE SAUCE

For me, it is the chocolate sauce that transforms the ice cream into a sundae, and this recipe, adapted from the one in Nigel Slater's *Real Food*, makes the best, the easiest, the tastiest and the poshest version I know.

MAKES ENOUGH FOR 6–8 SUNDAES

180 g good dark chocolate
50 g butter
50 g caster sugar
2 tablespoons golden syrup
175 ml milk

1. Break the chocolate into squares.
2. Melt the chocolate and butter in a bowl set over a pan of hot water.
3. Add the sugar and golden syrup and stir until dissolved.
4. Pour in the milk and mix in thoroughly.
5. Cook gently until the sauce thickens. Take off the heat and allow to cool a little before serving.

The sauce will thicken if it is left to cool completely. If you wish, it can be stored in the fridge – when it is cold and thick it is perfect for dipping strawberries in for a quick and delicious pudding.

PHOEBE'S EVEN POSHER ICE CREAM SUNDAE

Sometimes, though, more is more, and Phoebe decided that the twelve-year-old Lily Ruggles would enjoy an even posher, more colourful sundae with all the trimmings. This is the kind of sundae that has layers of different ingredients so that you are never quite sure what your long-handled spoon will reach. The recipe is pure child's play.

MAKES 1 SUNDAE

Fresh fruit (strawberries, raspberries, blueberries, nectarines, peaches or pineapple all work well)
2–3 scoops good vanilla ice cream (or your favourite flavour)
Chocolate sauce (as above)
Freshly whipped double cream
Sprinkles, such as hundreds and thousands
Glacé or maraschino cherries (optional)
1 wafer
1 paper umbrella

1. Put a few slices or pieces of fruit in the bottom of a tall ice-cream sundae glass, then a scoop of ice cream, then some sauce and more fruit, then another scoop of ice cream.
2. Pour on the chocolate sauce and finish with a generous whirl of cream.
3. Decorate with hundreds and thousands, a wafer, cherries if liked and a paper umbrella.

KIND AND
THOUGHTFUL TREATS

I think baking possesses a special power: as a simple, warm, heartfelt gesture of appreciation, affection or thoughtfulness it cannot be beaten.

The thing about baking is that you don't need to go for a *grand geste* to make an impact. Simple little sugar biscuits like those made for Maria by Marmaduke Scarlet and left each night in her bedroom in *The Little White Horse* make her feel "warm and happy… to find herself so cared for". An extra-extra-light meringue as a thank you for helping Cook tells Snubby that she appreciates his efforts. Anticipating a child's appetite for jam scones or preparing a special dish such as Pollyanna's calf's-foot jelly as a peace offering and a wake-up call to be glad again, speak of small efforts with big effects.

No matter how dated they may sometimes seem, the classic stories of childhood teach us that lavish, expensive gifts aren't always the best. Taking the time to make something, and having great time doing so, is often vastly more rewarding and enjoyable for both the donor and the recipient.

The kind and thoughtful treats I have included here are the ones made on genuine and caring occasions. There is nothing controlling or sinister or wheedling or ingratiating, no hint of the witch in Hansel and Gretel or the wicked queen in Snow White. Just a lovely sharing of treats made with care and affection.

For other thoughtful treats in this book see Ma's Pancake Men (page 22); Ma's Hand-Sweetened Cornbread (page 112); Pursey's Comforting Boiled Eggs (page 20); Joanna OBCBE's Ginger Biscuits (page 107); A Funny and Delightful Supper (page 94); Debby's Jumbles (page 105).

POLLYANNA'S
CALF'S-FOOT JELLY

Even if they refuse to play, I think most people can understand Pollyanna's 'glad game' as described and demonstrated in the eponymous novel by Eleanor H. Porter. It's not difficult, it doesn't require any screens, boards, counters or dice, and is simply a matter of looking on the bright side, even if we can't all emulate Pollyanna's "overwhelming, unquenchable gladness for everything".

With her positive, unselfconscious outlook, Pollyanna is a wonderful nurse, cheering up the town's previously negative, cantankerous and grumpy invalids, and she always enters sickrooms bearing bowls of calf's-foot jelly. This intrigued me, because even though I grew up in north-west England, the heartland of the UCP empire (combined shops and restaurants owned by United Cattle Products, with steamed-up windows, huge displays of tripe, and a strange smell of boiled cow) I was never given calf's-foot jelly when I was poorly.

Calf's-foot jelly used to be a well-known restorative and an invalid food, commonplace in the days when no part of a cow could be wasted, and even now many cultures still consider this reduction of caring thoughtfulness as the ultimate gesture of kindness. Making it is a labour of love and, as Pollyanna so ably shows, it should be made not out of duty but out of genuine care and interest. In order for it to be fully efficacious it should, of course, be both offered and accepted with a good seasoning of gladness.

I had every intention of testing this recipe, but it would seem that nowadays calves' feet are as rare as hen's teeth. All the butchers I contacted were unable to get hold of any, so I was forced to consider what a modern-day Pollyanna might offer in bowls to console, cheer and restore – and the answer was chicken soup. Home-made chicken soup has acquired an almost mythical status which can be attributed to its principal ingredient – the kindness and thoughtfulness with which it is made – which makes it a perfect alternative to calf's-foot jelly.

However, I want to share a recipe for the latter for the sake of keeping an old foodstuff alive, and because I feel sure that all the calves' feet in the world do not disappear completely. And I'm also giving a recipe for chicken soup; partly because I have bowed to pressure from people who are disgusted by the idea of the jelly, and partly because the ingredients are readily available.

CALF'S-FOOT JELLY
2 calf's feet

1. Scald the feet so that the hair can be removed. Slit in two and remove and discard the fat between the claws. Wash well in warm water.
2. Place both feet in a large pan with 3.5 litres water and bring slowly to the boil. Remove all scum as it rises.
3. When the liquid is well-skimmed, simmer gently for 6–7 hours until the liquid has reduced by half.
4. Strain into a large bowl if you are going to use the jelly for a sweet jelly, or into small, invalid-size bowls if you are serving it to invalids.
5. Put in a cool place to set.
6. Serve with a Pollyanna-ish smile.

A MODERN POLLYANNA'S CHICKEN SOUP

1 medium-size, free-range chicken
2 organic carrots, cut into quarters
2 celery sticks, cut in half
1 large onion, peeled and cut in half
4 bay leaves
10 peppercorns
2 teaspoons salt
Chicken strips and/or noodles or vermicelli and/or chopped parsley, to serve
(optional)

1. Put all the ingredients in a large solid pan.
2. Add enough water to just cover the chicken.
3. Bring to the boil, then turn down the heat and leave to simmer gently for 2 hours.
4. Taste and adjust the seasoning and strain the liquid.
5. You can serve the soup immediately, either plain or with strips of chicken and/or thin noodles or vermicelli pasta and/or chopped parsley. Or you can leave the soup to cool and reheat it as necessary, with or without additions.

Miss Heliotrope's Preferred Nice, Plain Junket

The Little White Horse is an enchanting book, and has been known to hold a spell over its readers for the rest of their lives. Its author, Elizabeth Goudge, is a master of detail and creates a book crammed with of rich descriptions of interiors, landscapes, nature, colours, textures and clothes. Most of all, though, I relish her utterly delicious details of food and cooking, which are some of the best I have encountered in children's literature.

The food is an endearing mix of old English, 1840s and 1940s, but focuses very much on traditional, home-made dishes and I was delighted to find that it includes junket, one of the puddings of my childhood. The very word 'junket' recalls the gentle, warm, spicy smell of the green nutmeg tin we had at home, and makes me think of the perfectly, glossily smooth, pale ivory, vanilla-flavoured desserts dusted with flecks of grated nutmeg that my mum used to make.

In The Little White Horse Miss Heliotrope suffers from indigestion and avoids rich food, unlike the rest of the characters with their extra-hearty appetites and heightened appreciation of Marmaduke Scarlet's superb cooking. So when he has made a huge syllabub for everyone else, he makes the perfect comfort food for someone with a delicate constitution: "a nice, plain junket, with a dash of brandy in it, and nutmeg on the top".

Junkets are in danger of becoming relics of the past, perhaps because the rennet that is used to curdle the fresh milk comes from a cow's stomach, and many consumers have a problem with that sort of closeness to the inner workings of farm animals. However, the good news is that vegetarian rennet is now widely available, so it is once again possible to reproduce the taste and texture of a delicately wobbly milky junket, flavoured with vanilla, rum or brandy, and sprinkled with nutmeg or cinnamon.

The milk must be heated to 'blood heat' (37°C) and it's important that it isn't too hot or too cool. If in doubt, use a thermometer.

SERVES 4–6
600 ml full-cream milk
1 tablespoon caster sugar
1 teaspoon rennet
1 teaspoon vanilla extract or 1 tablespoon rum or brandy
Nutmeg or ground cinnamon

1. Heat the milk and sugar in a pan then pour the mixture into a serving bowl. Gently stir in the rennet and the vanilla or the rum or brandy.
2. Leave the junket to set undisturbed at room temperature for 2 hours, then grate nutmeg or sprinkle cinnamon over the surface.
3. Serve at room temperature.

MISS DIMITY'S
JAM SCONES

There are no arguments about scones in children's literature. Instead of wasting time discussing the correct pronunciation of the word, the children simply get on with the far more enjoyable task of eating them. If there are any variations on the theme, it's whether they are best with butter or honey or jam.

Scones are an indoor, afternoon treat. They can't be made successfully in a cave or over a camp fire, so they are what returning adventurers and explorers scramble to eat when they reach a warm, aroma-filled kitchen or high-tea table after the rigours of tree-climbing and code-cracking. Since they are best enjoyed fresh and in lavish quantities, scones require an indulgent cook, nanny or mother who is prepared to bake to order.

Miss Dimity is one such housekeeper who accommodates Mike, Nora, Jack and Peggy during their parent-free summer in Enid Blyton's *The Secret of Spiggy Holes*. We know all will be well with their stomachs during this holiday from the first "splendid tea" she provides "… with three kinds of home-made cakes, and some delicious honey made by Miss Dimity's own bees… and big mugs of cold creamy milk".

But Miss Dimity's trump card for the affections of her charges is her wonderful "jam-scones". By chapter four the children have scented adventure and are busy discussing an enigmatic stranger, but they are not too preoccupied to rush down for scones when tea is announced, shouting, "is there cream with them?"

"There was. Dimmy poured out their milk and handed the new scones thickly spread with raspberry jam."

Not a single scone is left at the end of a silent tea.

"'You made too few scones, Dimmy dear,' said Jack, getting up.

"'Oh, no I didn't', said Dimmy. 'You ate too many!' I am just wondering whether I shall bother to think about supper for you – I am sure you couldn't possibly eat any more today.'"

The children laughed. They knew Dimmy was only teasing them."

Scones are easy to make and best eaten fresh, preferably within minutes of being taken out of the oven. They are wonderful with butter or honey, whipped or clotted cream. But, as Miss Dimity knows, they are best with cream and raspberry jam.

If necessary, the ingredients in the recipe can be doubled.

MAKES 9 SCONES

250 g self-raising flour

Pinch of salt

1 heaped dessertspoon caster sugar

A handful of sultanas (optional)

75 g butter (not too cold and hard)

1 large egg

2–3 tablespoons milk

Clotted cream or whipped double cream, butter, jam and honey, to serve

Baking tray, lined with baking parchment

1. Preheat the oven to 220°C/Gas Mark 7.
2. Sift the flour and salt into large mixing bowl. Stir in the sugar and the sultanas, if using.
3. Rub the butter into the mixture until it resembles fine breadcrumbs.
4. Beat the egg in a small bowl with 2 tablespoons of the milk.
5. Make a well in the centre of the dry mixture and pour in the egg and milk mix.
6. With a fork, and working quickly, bring the ingredients together, adding more milk if necessary to make the dough damp.
7. Form the dough into a ball and place on a floured work surface. Roll out quickly and gently until the dough is approximately 2.5 cm thick.
8. Shape into a rough square and cut into nine smaller squares, or use a cutter to make round scones.
9. Place the scones well apart on the tray and bake for 10–15 minutes until they are well risen and golden on top.
10. Transfer the tray to a wire rack and allow the scones to cool slightly for 5 minutes. Serve warm, with butter, jam, honey and cream.

SARA'S WARMING
CURRANT BUNS

With its tale of Sara Crewe's journey from riches to rags and back again, *A Little Princess* by Frances Hodgson Burnett is an Edwardian Cinderella story with the exciting additions of a melodramatic plot, a heartless schoolmistress, snobby and sneaky schoolgirls, kind and generous heroes and heroines, cold garrets, hidden suffering and overt moral messages. It's the kind of book that doesn't fade after reading, but continues to tug on the heart strings for a lifetime.

After her father dies, poor Sara Crewe is shut out of the life to which she once belonged. She can only see the happy Large Family from the outside and catch glimpses of their cosy, warm, well-lit family life through the window of their house. She can only press her nose against the bright, delicious-smelling bakery and fantasise about eating warm currant buns, the epitome of all that is comforting and nourishing and all that's missing from her sad, lonely life as a skivvy at the Young Ladies' Seminary where she was once regarded as a little princess.

Then, one day, she finds a silver fourpenny piece in the gutter and, on looking up, she sees the baker's shop opposite where "a cheerful, stout, motherly woman with rosy cheeks was putting into the window a tray of delicious newly baked hot buns, fresh from the oven – large, plump, shiny buns, with currants in them." The shop is warm, the penny currant buns smell delicious, and the kind baker gives Sara six instead of four. But instead of eating all of them herself, she gives five to a beggar girl who is even hungrier and needier than she is. And it is then that we know, without a doubt, that Sara is a true princess.

Currant buns are one of the best known of all children's treats and appear regularly in books throughout the twentieth century. Characters rich and poor enjoy them fresh, stale, warm, cold, from paper bags or from pockets, at home, at school, for teas, picnics or suppers, and always with gusto and satisfaction. They are sweetly and simply delicious, and deserve to be made in kitchens once again.

So here's a recipe for a classic currant bun to warm your body and soul. And to test the generosity and selflessness of any princess.

These currant buns could also be called sticky buns, that other staple of children's books. Made with or without the currants, they would pass muster with Snubby in Enid Blyton's Barney 'R' Mysteries, who is a frequenter of 'bun tents' (at events such as fairs and circuses) where sticky buns and lemonade are to be purchased and enjoyed.

MAKES 12 LARGE, PLUMP, SHINY BUNS

250 ml milk

15g fresh yeast or 1 dessertspoon
    dried yeast

1 teaspoon runny honey or caster sugar

500–550 g strong white flour

10 g sea salt

40 g caster sugar

60 g butter

2 eggs, beaten

Oil, for greasing

120 g currants

3 tablespoons caster sugar

Jam and/or butter, to serve (optional)

Baking tray, lined with baking parchment

1. Warm the milk until it is lukewarm/blood heat. It should not be too hot.
2. Put the yeast and honey or caster sugar in a bowl, and add the milk. Stir well to mix. Leave to bubble while you prepare the rest of the ingredients. If the mixture does not start to froth this is because the yeast is no longer alive, and you will have to start again with new yeast.
3. Put 500 g of the flour and the salt and sugar in a large mixing bowl. Stir with your hand to mix the ingredients.
4. Add the butter and rub it into the dry ingredients until the mix resembles fine breadcrumbs.
5. Pour in the milk and yeast mix, add the eggs and mix well with one hand. If the mixture is very sticky (too sticky to knead), add a little flour but not too much. This is a very well-behaved dough and will soon become manageable when you begin to knead it.
6. Turn the dough out on to a floured work surface and knead gently for 5–7 minutes until it becomes elastic and smooth. Form into a ball.
7. Lightly grease the mixing bowl with oil. Return the dough to the bowl, cover with clingfilm and leave to rise in a warm spot for 2–3 hours until it has doubled in size.
8. Preheat the oven to 200°C/Gas Mark 6.
9. Punch down the dough (deflate it with a floured hand) and turn it on to a floured work surface. Sprinkle the currants over the dough and knead gently to incorporate them.
10. Weigh the dough and divide it into twelve equal pieces. Roll each piece into a ball and place on the baking tray, close together but not touching. Cover with clingfilm and leave to rise for 30–45 minutes.

11. Bake for 20 minutes until the buns are golden brown and sound hollow when tapped on the base. Towards the end of baking, make the glaze by bringing the caster sugar and 3 tablespoons water to boiling point in a small pan.

12. Remove the tray from the oven and put on a wire rack. Brush the buns immediately with the glaze.

13. These buns are wonderful when warm. Eat as they are or with jam and/or butter.

COOK'S SPECIAL
SUGAR BISCUITS

The sugar biscuit has all but disappeared from view in the United Kingdom, yet characters in children's literature are still happily nibbling them, not realising for one moment that readers might wonder what these little treats are. Here is an example of a typically throwaway reference to this mysterious biscuit: in *The Ragamuffin Mystery* the Lynton children are off for a holiday in a caravan with Miss Pepper but, of course, they can't set off empty-handed:

"Diana and Roger said goodbye to their cheery old cook, and she pressed a bag into their hands. 'Just a few of my special sugar-biscuits to keep you going till dinner-time,' she said."

Sugar biscuits are the kind of biscuit you want to find on your pillow at bedtime, like a little whisper to say that someone has been thinking of you. In *The Little White Horse* Maria discovers sugar biscuits in her bedroom; one might be round with a pink sugar rose on top, another might be long and decorated with a green shamrock. Imagine how delightful it would be to have a whole series of night-time messages sent via sugar biscuits, and how much more exciting and delicious this would be than emails.

As you can see, I am completely taken by the sound of sugar biscuits. There is something fairylike and delicate about the name, and I would expect them to be the lightest, crispiest, most ethereal biscuit in the tin. To my mind, they should be child-friendly, sweet, thin and buttery, and with a deliciously crunchy, sugary surface. So I'm sure you will understand how intensely disappointed I was when, after reading so many stories that featured sugar biscuits, I couldn't find a single recipe.

And then I understood that the reason was that each home cook would have had her own, personal recipe because sugar biscuits are just simple, plain biscuits with a scattering of sugar on top. But if you are going to the trouble of making biscuits, they might as well taste delicious, and this recipe, adapted from a recipe by Jane Grigson combines simplicity and refinement. Make the dough well in advance of baking – six hours or the day before.

MAKES 40–50 BISCUITS
250 g soft butter
250 g caster sugar, plus extra for sprinkling
1 egg, lightly beaten
1 tablespoon double cream
300–330 g plain flour
½ teaspoon salt
1 teaspoon baking powder
Grated lemon or orange zest / vanilla extract / caraway seeds (optional)

2 baking trays lined with baking parchment.

1. In a large mixing bowl, cream the butter and sugar until pale and fluffy. Beat in the egg and the cream.
2. Sift in 300 g of the flour and the salt and baking powder, and add any flavouring, if using.
3. Mix well to make a light dough, adding a little more flour if the dough is too sticky to handle.
4. Bring the dough together into a ball. Divide the ball in two and on a lightly floured work surface quickly roll each half into a thick roll (approximately 5 cm in diameter) if you are going to make simple, round biscuits, or a flattish ball if

you are planning to roll out the dough and cut it into shapes. Wrap in clingfilm and put in the fridge to chill.

5. Preheat the oven to 180°C/Gas Mark 4. Cut the roll into thin slices with a sharp knife. Alternatively, roll the ball of dough out on a lightly floured work surface and cut into shapes with cutters. Place the rounds or shapes on the baking tray.

6. Scatter caster sugar over the biscuits.

7. Bake the biscuits for 6–8 minutes, depending on their thickness, until they are pale gold. Do not allow them to brown. Transfer the trays to a wire rack and leave the biscuits to cool.

Cook's Immensely Enjoyable Meringues

I'd never thought of meringues as a form of currency until I read *The Rilloby Fair Mystery* by Enid Blyton. Early in the story Snubby is desperate for Cook to make him some of his favourite meringues, so the two of them barter; he agrees to fetch a heavy roller for her mangle and carry out various other errands, and in return she makes some of her ethereally light meringues.

Meringues are their way of trading and showing affection; she lets Snubby have three, but Roger and Diana who have not earned as many, only receive two. "[They] enjoyed Cook's meringues immensely. They wished there were far, far more."

As with any Enid Blyton book, the more the pace of the story quickens the less eating there is (although meringues do reappear from time to time as a light and light-hearted culinary motif), so by the time the mystery has been solved it suddenly dawns on the children that they are starving.

"'Gosh – do you know we've never had any tea?' said Snubby in an injured voice. 'Would you believe it? No wonder I feel jolly hungry.'"

And so does the reader. Everyone is rewarded with an enormous meal which inevitably includes cook's immensely enjoyable meringues.

Meringues are like little clouds that condense into sticky pools of sweetness in your mouth; no wonder Snubby loves them. Despite the fact that Cook trades on her meringue-making skills, they are not difficult to make. I use golden rather than white caster sugar to obtain beautiful ivory meringues with the slightest hint of toffee. Allow 60 g sugar to one egg white.

MAKES APPROX. 30 MERINGUES
4 egg whites, at room temperature
240 g caster sugar
Whipped cream and fresh fruit, to serve

1 or 2 large baking trays, lined with baking parchment or silicone sheets

1. Preheat the oven to 140°C/Gas Mark 2.
2. In a very clean, large mixing bowl whisk the eggs whites until they stand in firm, creamy, satiny peaks.
3. Add half the sugar and whisk until glossy and smooth.
4. Add the remaining sugar and fold in thoroughly with a large metal spoon.
5. You can now pipe the mixture into small circles about 8 cm in diameter, but I find it quicker and easier to simply spoon it on to the tray(s) using a dessertspoon. Gently push into the desired shape.
6. Bake for approximately 50–60 minutes until the meringues are firm and dry (check the underside of one of them to make sure).
7. Transfer the tray(s) to a wire rack and leave the meringues to cool.
8. Serve with whipped cream and fresh fruit (raspberries, strawberries, blueberries, redcurrants, nectarines, peaches).

GROWING-UP

This section features some of those classic childhood treats best enjoyed either alone or with other children. They are closely connected to a desire to escape from reality and the world of adults to a place where children can assert their independence, feel grown-up and acquire a degree of sophistication. These are treats which can be taken from home and eaten in hidden places – in woods, attics, sheds, tree houses and barns.

A 'no adults allowed' treat might be something as simple as a crunchy apple to eat with a wonderful book, or as special as a paradise pie to accompany a discussion of daydreams and ambitions. Or it might be a treat disguised as a punishment, such as Bruce Bogtrotter's chocolate cake which is eaten to win peer group approval, or it may be delicious food eaten in secret by Colin and Mary in *The Secret Garden* in order to defy and confound adult expecations.

Occasionally though, it takes an adult to show a child the way to imagine a different world; Pauline's outlook expands with every sip of the exotic hot ginger drink made by Doctor Jakes. Or sometimes the treat is to to be left alone in the kitchen without an adult. Milly-Molly-Mandy, Little-Friend-Susan and Billy Blunt all qualify to be in this section with their Fried Onions (see page 78) but the undisputed young queen of the kitchen is Pippi Longstocking who lives on her own and can therefore bake as much, as often and whenever she likes – with wonderful results.

All children need space for their imagination to grow and flourish, and space to be themselves, and a little private space to enjoy private eating pleasures because there are some things, like the contents of pockets, that children need to keep secret from adults.

For more treats to be enjoyed in private or with other children, see Muvver's Lid Potatoes (page 81); Just Coconut Kisses (page 210); Real Dairy Ices (page 212); Amy's Pickled Limes (page 142); Tuck-Box Treats (page 134); Marvellous Midnight Feasts (page 144); Debby's Jumbles (page 105); Easy-Peasy Lemon-Squeezy Lemonade (page 190); Gorgeous Ginger Beer (page 193); Swallows and Amazons Seed Cake (page 134); The Swallows' Squashed-Fly Biscuits (page 162).

Attics And Apples

"'Jo! Jo! where are you?' cried Meg, at the foot of the garret stairs. 'Here!' answered a husky voice from above; and, running up, Meg found her sister eating apples and crying over the *Heir of Redclyffe*, wrapped up in a comforter on an old three-legged sofa by the sunny window. This was Jo's favourite refuge; and here she loved to retire with half a dozen russets and a nice book."

There is a very close connection between eating and reading, consuming both food and the written word, that makes the marriage of the two activities quite heavenly. Which means that there is sometimes nothing better in the whole world than escaping from everyone, disappearing to a favourite hideaway and holing up with food and books to nourish body and soul. When I read about Jo in her garret (where she not only reads, but later also writes, books) I immediately want to retreat to a quiet place, open my copy of *Little Women* and begin on a pile of crisp, russet apples to accompany my reading and crying.

The more I think about it, the more I realise that the self-contained, easy-to-eat apple is, perhaps, the ultimate food to enjoy with books. And Louisa May Alcott is right to give Jo a supply of russets, for a good book deserves a good apple and it is generally agreed that russet apples are some of the finest eating apples of all.

Rather than being a single variety, a 'russet' is a type of apple that 'russets' or turns greenish, golden brown, and develops a rough, uneven surface as as it ripens. Within the group there is a number of varieties such as Egremont Russet, Rosemary Russet, Golden Russet, Adam's Pearmain, St Edmund's Pippin and many more. It's possible to find some of these in supermarkets, but if you want to have enough apples to see you through your winter and spring reading it is best to pick your own and store them the old-fashioned way.

1. Pick apples in September and October.
2. Find a good pick-your-own farm via the internet or visit Brogdale Horticultural Trust, home of the National Fruit Collections.
3. Pick only unblemished fruit that is in perfect condition.
4. Place gently in a container, taking care to avoid bruising during picking and transportation.
5. Wrap each apple loosely in newspaper.
6. Place in layers in boxes or in a single layer on slatted wooden trays.
7. Keep in a cool, dry, dark, airy place such as a garage, barn or shed.
8. Make available to all readers in barns, sheds, attics, lofts, summer houses, tree houses, dens and hideways

Proper-Meeting
Rock Buns

When they were little, I read all sixteen Secret Seven books, one after the other, to Tom, Alice and Phoebe. I like to think they taught us all we need to know about clue-collecting, code-breaking and mystery-solving and, of course, how to run a secret club.

When it comes to the last point, it is clear that there is one golden rule and this is to provide food for the meetings. As Peter and Janet agree in *Secret Seven Win Through*, "Meetings weren't proper meetings, somehow, unless there was plenty to eat and drink while they talked."

So the seven sleuths cater for their shed meetings in a way that would put City businesses to shame. The meetings in the books feature, variously, sandwiches, jammy buns, doughnuts, chocolate cake, jam sponge, ginger biscuits, peppermint rock, apples, chocolate biscuits, jam tarts, ginger buns, oatmeal biscuits, boiled sweets, honey sandwiches, bags of toffees, bars of mint chocolate, gingerbread, currant buns warm from the oven, Janet's home-made lemonade and enormous jugs of cocoa.

For me, however, there is one quintessential Secret Seven meeting treat, and that is the rock bun, even if Janet and Peter's mother does have a somewhat cavalier attitude towards them. When Janet and Peter ask her for some food for a meeting, she says, "I'll give you lemons and some sugar, and you can make your own lemonade... and you can go and see if there are any rock-buns left in the tin in the larder. They'll be stale, but I know you don't mind that!"

Indeed they don't, and the buns pass muster with the children who know that a stale rock bun is better than no rock bun at all.

But a lovely, fresh, home-made rock bun is even better. It can be the most sub-lime treat – like a cross between a fruit cake and a scone, but much greater than the sum of the two parts. I've been baking rock buns for years in the hope that someone will ask me to join their club (and I have yet to encounter a stale one in the tin).

MAKES 12 ROCK BUNS

340 g plain flour
2 level teaspoons baking powder
¼ teaspoon salt
¼ nutmeg, freshly grated
175 g soft brown sugar
175 g soft butter
85 g sultanas

85 g raisins
85 g glacé cherries, halved
Finely grated zest of 1 lemon
(unwaxed)
1 large egg
1–2 tablespoons milk

Large baking tray, lined with baking parchment

1. Preheat the oven to 180°C/Gas Mark 4.
2. Sift the flour, baking powder, salt and nutmeg into a large bowl. Stir in the sugar and add the butter. Rub in the butter until the mix resembles fine breadcrumbs and feels sandy. Stir in the dried fruit and the lemon zest.
3. Whisk the egg and 1 tablespoon of the milk together. Make a well in the centre of the dry mixture and add egg and milk. Mix quickly with a fork. If the mixture is too dry and crumbly add a little more milk, but be careful not to make the mixture too slack or it will turn into cookies. It should come quickly to a stiffish dough; one of the tricks with rock buns is not to handle the ingredients too much.
4. Using your hands (my preferred method) or two forks, pile the mixture into 12 individual 'rocks' on the tray.
5. Bake for 15∕20 minutes until the buns are golden brown with the tiniest hint of squishiness on top. They will continue to cook when you have taken them out of the oven.
6. Transfer the tray to a wire rack and leave the buns to cool (although, it has to be said, they are just delicious when still a little warm).

KATY'S PARADISE
PICNIC PIE

It's funny how children can often miss the improving messages in so many well-meaning books. *What Katy Did* by Susan Coolidge made a huge impression on me, but I'm afraid the *Pilgrim's Progress* moral went right over my head. I was too busy reliving in my imagination Katy's terrible accident and rooting for her recovery to realise just how tamed and *improved* she had become. (And wondering why so many characters in late Victorian literature broke their backs, like Katy, or their legs and/or were confined to wheelchairs and beds.)

I was also sidetracked by the food. Long before the real drama happens, Katy and her brothers and sisters go to the place they call 'Paradise' for a never-to-be-repeated summer picnic. 'Paradise' is a marshy thicket beyond the symbolic gate (no doubt modelled on the 'Wicket Gate' in the *Pilgrim's Progress*) where the children decorate a tiny and very private 'bower' or den, just large enough for them, their two food baskets and their kitten. The afternoon turns into one of pure, unadulterated childish happiness:

"First came a great many ginger cakes... buttered biscuit came next – three apiece, with slices of cold ham laid in between; and last of all were a dozen hard-boiled eggs, and a layer of thick bread and butter sandwiched with corned beef... Oh, how good everything tasted in that bower... no grown-up dinner-party ever had so much fun."

And it doesn't stop there because this really is paradise, so there must be some paradise pies:

"... and there – oh, delightful surprise – were seven little pies – molasses pies, baked in saucers – each with a brown top and crisp, candified edge, which tasted like toffee and lemon-peel, and all sorts of good things mixed up together. There was a general shout... a tumult of joy... in an incredibly short time every vestige of pie had disappeared, and a blissful stickiness pervaded the party."

In their "blissful stickiness" the children discuss what they want to do with their lives, and Katy describes the many ways in which she will be "an ornament to the family". It's a perfect, crystallised moment and, as it turns out, the awful pride before her fall.

The description of those molasses pies lingers on the taste buds of the imagination long after the picnic, long after Katy's swing breaks, long after her suffering and redemption. The pies embody the sweetness and mix of good things in this idyllic picnic; they are most definitely celebratory rather than improving and are definitely worth preserving and making.

Since molasses does not play a huge part in British baking, I've decided to adapt the treat slightly to make a 'paradise pie' and have used molasses sugar (available in supermarkets) and lemon peel to make a paradise version of the classic American sugar pie. This recipe makes one large pie, but it would work well as smaller pies baked in individual pie tins. I make the pastry by hand as I don't have a food processor.

MAKES 1 PIE (SERVES 8)
170 g plain flour
1 tablespoon icing sugar
85 g butter
Grated zest of 1 lemon (unwaxed), plus lemon juice to mix (optional)
1 egg yolk

FOR THE FILLING:
200 g molasses sugar or soft dark brown sugar
1 lemon (unwaxed)
40 g plain flour
Pinch of salt
350–400 ml double cream
Nutmeg, to grate

22-cm tart or pie tin, greased with butter

1. Sift the flour and icing sugar into a large bowl. Add the butter and rub it in until the mix resembles fine breadcrumbs.
2. Stir in the lemon zest, then add the egg yolk and 2 teaspoons lemon juice or water. Mix with a knife or your hand, adding tiny amounts of liquid as necessary to bring the dough together into a ball. Add as little liquid as possible.
3. Shape the dough into a flattish round, cover it in clingfilm and chill it in the fridge for 30 minutes, or until you are ready to use it.
4. Preheat the oven to 180°C/Gas Mark 4.
5. Roll the dough out on a floured surface and carefully line the tin with it; make sure you cover the sides of the tin right up to the top edge as the pastry will shrink a little during baking. Prick the base a few times with a fork, cover the whole case

with foil and place a layer of dried beans on the base (to stop the pastry rising up).

6. Bake for 15 minutes, take the pastry case out of the oven and remove the beans and foil, then return the pastry to the oven to bake for another 5 minutes or until it is pale gold and dry.

7. Meanwhile, to make the filling, put the sugar in a mixing bowl and grate the zest of the lemon over it.

8. Sift in the flour and salt. Mix with a fork or your fingers, breaking up any lumps in the sugar until you have a fine, crumbly mix..

9. When the pastry case is cooked, tip in the filling mix and spread it evenly over the base.

10. Measure out 350 ml of the cream in a Pyrex jug and warm it slightly.

11. Pour the cream over the filling mix until the pastry case is almost but not quite full. Add more cream if necessary to bring it to the correct level.

12. Bake for 35–45 minutes until the surface starts to turn brown. Remove and leave to cool on a wire rack. The filling will initially appear quite runny, but it will set as the pie cools.

Pippi Longstocking's Heart-Shaped Swedish Ginger Snaps

Pippi Longstocking might be thin and only nine years old, but she has colossal energy and focus, and she never does things by halves. Take, for example, baking, for Pippi is an enthusiastic and accomplished baker with a brilliantly unorthodox style.

She has no concept of restraint and doesn't bother with the usual kitchen rules, so when she decides to bake ginger snaps, she doesn't make a dozen or two but five hundred, and rolls and cuts out the enormous quantity of heart-shaped biscuits on the kitchen floor, "'Because you know what?... What good is it to roll the dough on the table when you're going to bake at least five hundred ginger snaps?'" How very practical, thinks the child. How very horrifying, thinks the adult.

Pippi's friends and next-door neighbours, Tommy and Annika, visit while she is baking and are spellbound by her almost magical skills:

"Pippi could certainly work fast! Tommy and Annika sat down on the fire-wood box to watch. She rolled out the ginger-snap dough, she tossed the biscuits on to the baking trays, and she flung the trays into the oven. They thought it was almost like watching a film."

And so, in a comically speeded-up Harold Lloyd- or Charlie Chaplin-style scene, she produces five hundred ginger snaps and then off she goes to look for "stuff" outside, and is delighted when she turns up a rusty old cake tin. "'What a find! What a real *find*! You can never have too many tins,'" she shouts.

How could you *not* love a girl like Pippi who bakes like fury, utters lines like this and gives old cake tins a new home? This is someone who cares deeply about good baking, so I'm quite sure her ginger snaps would be delicious.

Pippi's Swedish ginger snaps are biscuits, and quite different to English ginger, or brandy, snaps. They are traditionally cut in a heart shape and on this point Pippi, for once, conforms. This recipe makes 40–50 thin biscuits, but the quantities can be multiplied by ten should you wish to make five hundred. Swedish ginger snaps are often beautifully decorated with patterns piped on with white icing. See Royal (Writing) Icing (page 272), should you wish to decorate yours.

MAKES 40–50 THIN GINGER SNAPS

8 cloves

8 cardamom pods

½ cinnamon stick or 1 teaspoon ground cinnamon

150 g sugar

2 tablespoons golden syrup

2 teaspoons ground ginger

85 g soft butter, cut into small pieces

300 g plain flour

1 teaspoon bicarbonate of soda

2 baking trays, lined with baking parchment

1. Measure out and grind the cloves, cardamom seeds and the cinnamon stick, if using.
2. Put the sugar, golden syrup, ground ginger, ground cinnamon if using, and the cloves and cardamom seeds in a medium pan with 4 tablespoons water and heat gently for 2–3 minutes until the sugar dissolves. Allow to cool for 5 minutes before transferring to a large mixing bowl.

3. With an electric whisk or wooden spoon, beat in the butter, adding the pieces gradually until the mix is smooth.

4. Sift in the flour and bicarbonate of soda and mix thoroughly to produce a sticky dough.

5. Divide the dough into two or three pieces, wrap in clingfilm and chill in the fridge for at least 2 hours or overnight.

6. When you are ready to bake, take the dough out of the fridge and allow it to warm up for a few minutes while you preheat the oven to 200°C/Gas Mark 5.

7. Roll out each piece of the dough with a wooden rolling pin on a floured surface (the floor, if it works for you). I find the best way to do this is to put a layer of clingfilm over the dough as this stops it sticking to the rolling pin. Roll the dough very thin and cut out biscuits with a heart-shaped cutter. Place well apart on a baking tray.

8. Bake for 8–10 minutes; take care not to let the biscuits burn.

9. Transfer the trays to a wire rack and leave the biscuits to cool. Ginger snaps turn crispy as they cool.

BRUCE BOGTROTTER'S HEROIC CHOCOLATE CAKE

Children's books have their fair share of unappetising, large children who are used by their creators to make statements about greed and rudeness and self-control (or lack thereof), and Roald Dahl's books contain an exceptionally high number of dire warnings. So it's not often that over-eating is seen as a heroic, self-determining act, and this makes Bruce Bogtrotter's cake-eating feat in *Matilda* all the more impressive.

Although Dahl himself loved chocolate he ate it in moderation and clearly disliked over-indulgence. But eating in order to defy a nasty, bullying teacher is of a

different order of chocolate-eating, and in this brilliant scene Dahl exploits the one area of control that children can exercise over adults – whether or not to accept or refuse food, or, as in this case, eat something in order to make a glorious statement of independence.

Bruce Bogtrotter is a cake thief and has stolen a slice of the chocolate cake belonging to the terrifying, bullying teacher, the Trunchbull, and his punishment is to be made to eat a huge, humiliating cake in front of the school. But Bruce Bogtrotter rises to the challenge and, far from melting away, his confidence grows with each slice until the children sense that he is winning an enormous battle with the Trunchbull. Finally, by dint of sheer willpower, cheered on by the children, he triumphs by eating the entire cake.

Not long ago Phoebe made an incredibly large, rich and filling chocolate cake for a birthday, and it occurred to me that this was exactly the kind of cake that Bruce Bogtrotter could eat on his own if pressed to defend himself. None of us could eat more than a slice or so – not even Tom's hungry teenage friends who declared it the best chocolate cake they'd ever tasted – and it was then that I understood just how brave Bruce Bogtrotter had been. So here is Phoebe's recipe for a heroic chocolate cake.

MAKES 1 VERY LARGE CAKE (SERVES 12—16)
350 g soft brown sugar
350 g soft butter
6 eggs
270 g self-raising flour
80 g good-quality cocoa powder
1 teaspoon baking powder
2–3 tablespoons milk
Chocolate buttons or Maltesers, to decorate (optional)

FOR THE FILLING AND TOPPING:

350 g icing sugar
115 g good-quality cocoa powder
150 g soft butter
3–4 tablespoons milk

26-cm round cake tin, greased with butter and lined with baking parchment

1. Preheat the oven to 180°C/Gas Mark 4.
2. In a large mixing bowl, cream the sugar and butter until light and fluffy.
3. Add the eggs to the mixture one at a time, beating well after each addition.
4. Measure out the flour, cocoa and baking powder in a bowl, then sift them into the large bowl. Fold in gently with a large metal spoon, adding enough milk to make the mixture smooth but not runny.
5. Spoon the mixture into the tin and level the surface.
6. Bake for 50–55 minutes until a metal skewer or sharp knife inserted in the cake comes out clean. Check the cake after 30 minutes and if necessary place a sheet of foil on top to prevent it burning.
7. Leave the cake in its tin on a wire rack to cool completely, then turn out.
8. To make the filling and topping, sift the icing sugar and cocoa powder into a large bowl and add the butter and 2 tablespoons of the milk. Mix well with a round-ended knife or electric whisk, adding more milk if necessary to make the butter icing soft and easy to spread. Taste, and adjust the flavour with more icing sugar or cocoa if necessary.
9. Carefully cut the cake into two layers. Spread a good quantity of the butter icing on the bottom layer, replace the top layer and cover the whole cake with the remaining icing. Arrange chocolate buttons and/or Maltesers on the topping, if using.

The Secret Appetite

Most hungry children in classic storybooks enjoy their food without inhibitions, and it is rare to find any youngsters deliberately refusing to eat in order to defy adults. But The Secret Garden *explores a very different aspect of children's appetites and self-control, and Frances Hodgson Burnett is brilliantly perceptive when it comes to the psychology of eating.*

At the beginning of the story, Mary and Colin are two privileged, cooped-up, bored and sickly children whose lives are apparently mapped out for them by a predetermined social code. They have become pale and etiolated, like neglected plants growing on poor soil in the shade, unlike the healthy, robust and vigorous Dickon who thrives on fresh air, exercise and plenty of light. Indeed, Mary and Colin appear to display anorexic tendencies in their refusal to eat in order to please adults; when Dr Craven sees an improvement in Colin's health and suggests writing to his father, Colin's immediate reaction is to vow to eat less so that he can fulfil is father's wish (as he sees it) that he would die.

But the problem for the two would-be hunger-strikers (whose planned method of obtaining rights and freedoms mirrors that of the contemporary suffragettes) is that the more time they spend in the secret garden, the more their appetites grow:

"… [Colin] made up his mind to eat less, but unfortunately it was not possible to carry out this brilliant idea when he wakened each morning with an amazing appetite and the table near his sofa was set with a breakfast of home-made bread and fresh butter, snow-white eggs, raspberry jam, and clotted cream. Mary always breakfasted with him, and when they found

themselves at the table – particularly if there were delicate slices of sizzling ham sending forth tempting odours from under a hot silver cover – they would look into each other's eyes in desperation."

The children find they cannot stop themselves eating because they are experiencing true hunger for the first time in their lives due to their new, gloriously creative, outdoor life. So they eat covertly and well away from the cook, doctor, nurse and the unpleasant Mrs Medlock, but secretly supplied by the marvellously nurturing Mrs Sowerby via her son Dickon, until they are full of life and energy and "cottage-made currant buns" and are consequently healthy in both mind and body.

The Secret Garden *could have been called* The Secret Appetite; the more the children are free to explore the world independently, instinctively and unfettered by adult expectations, the more they discover their true appetites for life. Frances Hodgson Burnett extols the virtues of freedom, fresh air and good food for growing children, no matter where they belong in the world – a message that is both timeless and, these days, increasingly timely.

For a recipe for Mrs Sowerby's currant buns see Sara's Warming Currant Buns (page 226).

ROBBER TEA

When you are a child, indoor dens are one of the highlights of the winter months. My children regularly adapted all the furniture in our lounge in order to create quite wonderful and ingenious dens from cushions and sheets and blankets and books. These would last for days, and parents were strictly forbidden to reconstruct the lounge after they had gone to bed.

Call me liberal or soft, but I would never have the heart to demolish a hospital/home/shop/outlaws' hidey-hole because I have such great memories of my own dens under my Nana's green baize card table. She would indulge me and my brother by covering it with thick blankets and would even rig up a red light bulb to hang from the 'ceiling' (unthinkable these days) which made it seem terribly exotic and far removed from the reality of the cold, wet Manchester outside. She would deliver supplies of food and drink to us, and then retire to her armchair and knit and read just as if we weren't there. A clever move, because the illusion would have been shattered if she'd reminded us of her presence.

So I enjoy the description of the children's robber tea in *The Box of Delights* by John Masefield – a game to be played on winter evenings in the old study. First, the children close the curtains and make sure the room is dark, then they build up the fire with wood and coal to make a good toasting fire. Next, they pull the table and some chairs over to the bookshelves, draping dark curtains over it and the chairs in order to make an inner cave. Finally, the cave is illuminated with lanterns that have coloured glass slides.

All that's needed now is a supply of "toasting forks, sausages, bread, butter, dripping and strawberry jam" and they can pretend they are robbers as they lie on the hearthrug in the glow of the fire toasting bread and sausages which they then take to eat in the cave. It's a wonderfully evocative scene that makes the whole idea of dens utterly irresistible.

Since all things dennish must, to a certain extent, remain instinctive and secret, I can't give a definitive recipe for a robber tea. But I can give some suggestions, which I hope can be approved, adapted and improved by young den-builders.

If you don't have a toasting fork (see Resources, page 298) you can always make one from wire coat-hangers. In fact, a home-made toasting fork fits in beautifully with the spirit of improvisation that is the essence of den-building.

MAKES 1 ROBBER TEA

1 toasting fork per person

*Waterproof sheet or tablecloth
    to protect the rug (even John
    Masefield includes this house-
    keeping detail)*

*Freedom to cook plus minimal adult
    supervision*

2–3 chipolata sausages per person

Fresh sliced bread

Butter

*Uncle Ambrose's Strawberry Jam
    (page 126)*

Honey, peanut butter

Dripping (optional)

Marshmallows

Cheese

Drinks

1. Build your den, then make and/or light fire.
2. Switch off the lights.
3. Toast and roast and pretend you are in another world.

Marilla's Zero-Alcohol Raspberry Cordial

Some children's books, like some foods, don't travel well from continent to continent. But L.M. Montgomery's *Anne of Green Gables* has never suffered from a trans-Atlantic gap, and it has captivated, charmed and amused readers both young and old all over the world. Anne's romantic flights of fancy, unstoppable talk and daily enjoyment of natural beauty are the stuff of legend. As is the hilarious chapter 'Diana is invited to Tea, with Tragic Results' which describes the tea party at which Anne gets her new best friend (aged eleven) drunk.

She and Diana, both wearing their *second*-best dresses, start out by observing the correct tea-party protocol. They take on the rôles of genteel, well-bred lady acquaintances, exchange pleasantries and are altogether proper and polite. They are to eat some of Marilla's wonderful fruit cake and cherry preserve and, best of all, enjoy something very special which begins with an 'r' and a 'c' and is bright red. Anne, with her new-found sophistication, claims airily, "I love bright red drinks, don't you? They taste twice as good as any other colour."

How easy it is to see in retrospect that red drinks might just spell danger.

So, after they have played in the orchard, Anne plies Diana with three glasses of what she thinks is raspberry cordial, but she herself abstains because she is full after eating apples. A wise move, as it turns out, for Anne has served Marilla's celebrated three-year-old currant wine and poor Diana is soon the worse for wear. But even after she has been taken to task by Diana's mother and banned from seeing her friend, the reader, like Marilla, is overcome by an "unholy tendency to laughter".

256

All the time I was reading the story of Anne's tea party, I was desperate to taste some proper, old-fashioned raspberry cordial. The very word is something we don't hear too often these days, yet real cordials are easy to make, and taste so much better than any commercial brand. With their jewel colours, lovely syrupy viscosity and concentrated flavours, they capture the essence of summer fruit and are wonderfully reviving on a hot day. And you can serve a cordial at a tea party to guests of any age, safe in the knowledge that it will not send them home intoxicated.

MAKES APPROX. 1 LITRE
600 g fresh raspberries
300 g caster sugar
Juice of 1 lemon
Still or sparkling mineral water and ice, to serve

1. Check the raspberries to make sure none are mouldy. Remove these and any bits of stalk and leaf.
2. Put the raspberries in a large pan. Add the sugar, lemon juice and 750 ml water.
3. Place on a medium heat and bring to the boil, stirring occasionally so that the sugar does not stick.
4. Simmer gently for 5 minutes.
5. Remove from the heat and leave to cool for a few minutes.
6. Strain the liquid into a bowl. Press down gently on the fruit pulp in the sieve to extract colour and flavour.
7. Leave to cool, then pour the cordial into glass bottles or a jug.
8. Store in the fridge and use within a couple of days.
9. Serve with still or sparkling mineral water and ice.

Doctor Jakes' Heavenly Hot Ginger Drink

"**P**auline, Petrova and Posy had a very ordinary nursery life."
It's rather difficult to swallow the opening line of the second chapter of *Ballet Shoes* by Noel Streatfeild, coming as it does after the magical, fairy-tale opening chapter which tells of the unusual way in which the three Fossil sisters are collected and brought to live in London by Great-Uncle Matthew. This is a unique, funny and enchanting start to a book, so the suggestion that the girls then have "an ordinary nursery life" comes as something of a disappointment.

Fortunately, it turns out that this is nothing more than a calm interlude, because it's not long before life with the Fossils does turn into an extraordinary story. And at the start of chapter three we get a delicious, spicy, perfumed whiff of what's to come.

Pauline has a cold, and is bored and miserable until she is invited into the room of Doctor Jakes, who is also suffering from a cold and is making a hot ginger drink to combat it, and she invites Pauline to join her.

Although Pauline doesn't recognise it fully at the time, this is the marvellous moment when the world of books and Shakespeare and drama opens up for her, when she begins to realise that she can make a name for herself, should she want to. It is fitting that her epiphany is accompanied by a delicious-smelling, mysteriously brewed hot drink; indeed, it is as if this is a magic potion that has the power to transform a young girl's life.

"Pauline sipped her drink. It was very hot, but simply heavenly – the sort of drink certain to make a cold better. She looked across at Doctor Jakes over the rim of her glass, her eyes shining.

'Do you suppose me and Petrova and Posy could make Fossil an important sort of name?

'Of course.'"

And, as it turns out, this hot ginger drink and encounter with a sophisticated, feminist, literary lady sets Pauline on the road to Hollywood. And life, generally, does not get less "ordinary" than that.

I think we could all do with the occasional glass of an exotic elixir to help open our eyes to the vast possibilities of life. Here is a recipe for a life-changing ginger drink. Of course, if your existence is already exciting and rewarding, it's also a great comfort when you have a common cold.

MAKES 300 ML (SERVES 2)
1 piece (approx. 25 g) fresh ginger
1 cinnamon stick
4 cardamom pods
Juice of ½ lemon
1–2 teaspoons runny honey

1. Put the kettle on and while you are waiting for the water to boil, peel and roughly chop the ginger. Place this and the cinnamon stick in a measuring jug.
2. Split the cardamom seeds with a sharp knife and add them to the jug. Add the lemon juice.
3. Pour boiling water over the spices up to the 300 ml mark, add the honey according to taste and stir well.
4. Strain and serve in little glasses or cups.
5. Alternatively, if you want more flavour, leave the drink to brew for 5–10 minutes before straining it, then reheat it gently in a small pan if necessary.

Pocket Cache

A pocket is the natural place to keep a treasure; it's safe and handy, and no one else knows what's in there. So the art of keeping a cache of sweet treats and important belongings in trouser pockets is one that many boys in books and reality have mastered with aplomb.

Take William, for example, hero of the stories by Richmal Crompton. If we turned out his pockets we would find a penknife, a piece of putty, a spinning top, pieces of string, plus some gooseberry eyes and a few biscuits, because you never know when you'll be hungry or marooned on a desert island.

Or Cyril in Five Children and It, *whose pockets hide biscuits mixed with a hank of twine, a few fir cones and a ball of cobbler's wax. These biscuits are happily discovered at a hungry moment and enjoyed by all, despite the interesting range of extra aromas and flavours that makes them taste "a little oddly".*

Or Jo in The Family From One End Street. *Jo keeps his private treats in his pockets – a currant bun and a bun sprinkled with white sugar – and carefully saves them for a whole day so that he can eat them when he hides in the cinema the next day. Neither William, whose sweets tend to emerge from his pockets in a rather mucky state, nor Jo whose buns melt and come out fluffy, are in the slightest bit put-out by the wear and tear that occurs to eatables when stored in pockets.*

Fatty, in the Five Find-Outer stories by Enid Blyton, is the king of well-equipped pockets and can be relied on to have just the right gadget for any adventure. Because he is partial to keeping toffee in his pockets (which, unusually, are never turned out by his mother) these often contain a piece or two, sometimes with a vital clue happily and stickily attached. Fatty's pockets also rattle with cash – this is the boy who is always ready to treat himself and others to buns, cocoa and ices.

And it's not just boys who like to have a pocket cache. One of my favourite moments when I was doing the research for this book was when I was reading The Swish of the Curtain *by Pamela Brown. The children, who go on to form their own theatre company, attend a potentially dreary meeting in the Ladies' Institute Hall, so Maddy (the book's gourmand) is delighted to discover a packet of pear drops in her knicker pocket. I'm sure the pocket was meant to hold a ladylike handkerchief, but I'd rather have a bag of sweets in my knicker pocket (or coat pocket, or trouser pocket) any day.*

TEMPTING TURKISH DELIGHT

If you have only ever read about it in *The Lion, the Witch and the Wardrobe*, Turkish delight must be one of the most difficult foods to imagine. What you know from the book is that it is sweet and delicious, presented in pretty boxes tied with silk ribbons, and that pieces can be picked up with fingers and eaten straight away because Edmund stuffs them into his mouth as fast as he can. But after this there is a huge gap in information; although it's clear that Turkish delight is the stuff of cravings and grown-up special treats, you still don't know how Turkish delight *tastes*.

So how to describe this sweetmeat? Well, it comes in cubes that a person less greedy than Edmund would need two or three bites to finish. These are dusted with a fine coating of icing sugar mixed with cornflour, so it is inevitable that you will end up with a light covering of sweet powder on your fingers and clothes after indulging. The texture is unique – firm, jelly-ish, sticky and lightly chewy. Good-quality Turkish delight melts in your mouth and fills it with an unmistakable flavour of scented rose petals. It's rather like eating a soft, fluffy powder puff with a whiff of perfume bottles and dressing tables.

Traditionally Turkish delight is made with sugar and starch and rosewater, but it also come in different flavours (lemon, mint, cardamom) and with additions such as nuts (pistachios, hazelnuts). For me, though, nothing beats the original musky pink rose variety and this is what the recipe below makes. I won't claim that the result has the authenticity of the genuine article, but it does offer a tantalising taste of the treat that tempts the weak-willed Edmund.

Turkish delight is also one of those sweets that is great fun to make at home, with lots of sugary stickiness and a strange-looking mixture. And there's nothing to stop you packaging yours in a smart, beribboned box that opens with a pretty white cloud of icing sugar and the promise of being pampered.

MAKES APPROX. 1.4 KG

900 g sugar

Juice of ½ lemon

250 g cornflour

1 teaspoon cream of tartar

1 ½ tablespoons rosewater

Pink or red food colouring

100 g icing sugar

Square (20 x 20 cm) baking tin, lightly oiled

1. Put the sugar in a large, heavy pan and add 300 ml water and the lemon juice.
2. Heat gently, stirring constantly, until the sugar dissolves.
3. Bring the syrup to the boil and simmer until the temperature reaches the soft-ball stage (114–118°C). That is, when a small amount of syrup is dropped into a bowl of cold water it forms a soft ball that can be squashed flat.
4. Remove the pan from the heat.
5. Put 225 g of the cornflour and the cream of tartar into a second large, heavy pan. Place on a medium heat and gradually add 700 ml of water, stirring all the time until there are no lumps.
6. Keep stirring as you bring the mix to the boil; it will form a very thick, gluey paste.
7. Now pour in the hot sugar syrup a little at a time, stirring well after each addition to mix thoroughly.
8. Reduce the heat and allow the mixture to cook very gently for 50–60 minutes

until it is pale golden. You will need to stir it frequently to prevent it sticking to the pan. It will become a very thick, sticky paste.

9. Remove the pan from the heat and add the rosewater and a small amount of food colouring to achieve the shade you desire. Mix thoroughly.

10. Transfer to the prepared tin and spread evenly.

11. Allow to stand at room temperature overnight.

12. The Turkish delight is now ready to be cut up and dusted. Sift the icing sugar and the remaining cornflour on to a work surface or large chopping board. Turn the Turkish delight out of the tin on to the dusting mix. With a sharp, oiled knife, cut it into 2-cm cubes. Roll the cubes in the icing sugar and cornflour mix to coat all sides.

13. Line a box or an airtight container with greaseproof paper dusted with the icing sugar and cornflour mix. Fill with layers of Turkish delight separated by sheets of dusted greaseproof paper.

If you would rather buy your Turkish delight, I find the best sort comes in wooden boxes and is imported from Turkey. It can be found in specialist food shops and delicatessens all year round, and in good supermarkets in the run-up to Christmas. Alternatively, Hotel Chocolat has a beautifully packaged box containing a variety of flavours (see www.hotelchocolat.co.uk).

Special
Occasions

A special occasion should be one to remember. So it is a source of great amusement and entertainment that events such as teas and parties in books are often
memorable for the wrong reasons, for bringing out the worst, and not the best,
behaviour in children. It seems that very few of them can live up to the expectations
of a big occasion; the pressure to behave well can be all too much, and it's at these
events that we see the great nonconformist characters such as Edmund Pevensie, Pippi
Longstocking, Bad Harry and My Naughty Little Sister at the height of their
challenging behaviour. Which is, of course, highly gratifying to the average, and
averagely behaved, young reader.

Fortunately for those interested in such matters, this waywardness is often
accompanied by delicious food and treats. The very fact that someone has gone to the
trouble of baking something special makes the children's defiance even more
deplorable – or impressive, depending on your point of view. It reminds me of Mary
Jane in A.A. Milne's poem and her tantrum when faced with "rice pudding again";
so often the grown-ups are unable to understand what's the matter, but the reader
always knows.

It's unsurprising then, that young readers love it when the adults themselves are
not on their best behaviour for these special occasions. Stationmaster Perks is less
than charming when faced with the kindness and generosity of the railway children
and villagers until he realises their birthday gifts are not charity, but tokens of
appreciation. At least he eventually relents and enjoys himself, unlike Mrs Persimmon in *Mary Poppins* who remains tight-lipped and disapproving of the uproarious

tea party fuelled by laughing gas, and refuses point-blank to inhale.

The recipes that follow are based on my favourite fictional special occasions, the ones that make me laugh and make me hungry at the same time. It's a wickedly irresitible combination.

For more treats for special occasions, see Pauline's Iced and Patterned Buns (page 123) and Royal (Writing) Icing (page 272) to go on birthday cakes.

MRS PERSIMMON'S
CRUMPETS

Crumpets are the backbone of any good afternoon tea party – even when the party is an extraordinary one, eaten at a table floating in the air while you take care not to bump your head on the ceiling.

Mr Wigg's birthday tea party in *Mary Poppins* appears at first to be very normal; it includes crumpets and there is nothing more solidly sensible and earth-bound than a good, old-fashioned English crumpet. When Jane and Michael enter Mr Wigg's large, cheerful room, they survey the scene:

"At one end of it a fire was burning brightly and in the centre stood an enormous table laid for tea – four cups and saucers, piles of bread and butter, crumpets, coconut cakes and a large plum cake with pink icing."

But it isn't long before this apparently ordinary tea party turns topsy-turvy due

to an uncontrollable excess of laughing gas. The participants float to the ceiling, eat their tea in the 'wrong' order – cake first, not sandwiches – and the adults behave like children. It is the epitome of a joyful tea party with good company, good food, lots of laughter and a complete and enjoyable loss of adult dignity.

Crumpets are the stuff of cold days, warm fires and toasting forks, and are soft, filling and comforting. So it is ironic that in this story they are made by the thin, disapproving and very dignified Mrs Persimmon, and the episode simply demonstrates how much she is missing out on in life when she refuses to rise to the occasion and join in with crumpets and laughter.

It's best to allow 2 ½–3 hours from starting the recipe to eating the hot crumpets.

MAKES APPROX. 18 CRUMPETS
1 dessertspoon dried yeast or 15 g fresh yeast
1 teaspoon runny honey
650 ml lukewarm milk and water (half and half)
230 g plain flour
230 g strong white flour
2 teaspoons salt
¾ teaspoon cream of tartar
½ teaspoon bicarbonate of soda
Oil, for greasing
Butter, jam, golden syrup, maple syrup or cheese, to serve

10-cm crumpet rings, well oiled; griddle or heavy-based frying pan, lightly oiled

1. Put the yeast into a medium bowl and add the honey and 500 ml of the lukewarm milk and water. Mix well until the yeast has dissolved into the liquid and the honey is mixed in. You should start to see little frothy bubbles appear on the

surface immediately; this is the good sign that your yeast is alive and well. If this doesn't happen, you will need to start again with a new batch of yeast.

2. In a large mixing bowl, mix the flours, salt and cream of tartar. Pour the yeasty liquid into the flour and mix well to make a thick, smooth batter. Cover with clingfilm or a damp tea towel and leave to stand in a warm place until the batter rises and its surface is covered with bubbles. This will take 1½–2 hours.

3. Dissolve the bicarbonate of soda in the remaining lukewarm milk and water and stir thoroughly into the batter. Leave in a warm place for a further 30–45 minutes, by which time the surface should once again be covered with little bubbles.

4. You are now ready to cook the crumpets. First, it's best to make sure your batter isn't too thick or too thin by cooking a test crumpet. If your batter is too thin and runs out from under the ring, add a little more flour to the mix. If small holes do not form on the surface your batter is too thick, in which case you need to add a little more water to loosen the mix.

5. Heat the griddle or frying pan over a moderate heat then place the rings on it. Spoon or ladle batter into each ring – it's up to you how thick you want your crumpets to be, but I find that slightly thinner ones, about 1 cm–1.5 cm thick, are best. Turn the heat up for a couple of minutes to ensure plenty of bubbles form, then reduce the heat and cook gently until the surface of the crumpet is dry and set, and covered with holes – this should take 5–8 minutes.

6 Now ease the rings off, flip the crumpets over and cook for a further 3 minutes; the holey side is meant to be paler and softer than the underside. The crumpets can be eaten immediately, or wrapped in a cloth or kept in a covered dish while you make more batches.

7. Crumpets are undeniably best when fresh and, to my mind, when served with medically dangerous amounts of butter. Home-made crumpets are best eaten fresh as they begin to go rubbery with age.

LOVEDAY'S MARRIAGE
PROPOSAL PARKIN

L ove stories can be simply yucky to young readers, so any marriage proposal in children's literature has to have an element that distracts from the squirmily embarrassing facts — and choking on parkin does the job wonderfully well.

In *The Little White Horse* Elizabeth Goudge is sufficiently sensible to make the occasion of the young teenage Robin's proposal to Maria a cosy, warm tea-time "with bread and butter, honey and cream, and golden-brown parkin" provided by Robin's mother, Loveday. The children eat hungrily but Robin misunderstands Maria when she tells him she is going to marry a boy from London:

"The parkin stuck in his gullet and he choked so violently that Loveday had to pat him on the back and pour him out a fresh cup of tea."

Maria knows he has misunderstood her and she waits demurely until the penny drops that *he* is the boy from London. The more controlled she is, the angrier he becomes, until his mother suggests that he goes down on one knee and proposes in a gentle voice. Thankfully, he and the reader are spared this humiliation when Maria quickly tells him she will marry him.

"'That's all right then,' he said with a great sigh of relief. 'That's settled. I'll have some more parkin, please, Mother.'"

Parkin is one of my all-time favourite baked treats from my northern childhood. I associate it with autumn, mists, bonfires and fireworks (it's a traditional Fifth of November speciality) rather than love scenes, but I can appreciate the masterful introduction of such a delicious, spicy and tasty diversion into this marriage proposal. And I applaud the way in which Robin's mind returns immediately to the parkin once the messy business of proposing has been concluded.

Parkin is a great cake-tin cake as it really does improve with keeping.

SERVES 8–1

1 x 454 g tin black treacle
125 g butter
140 ml milk
125 g soft brown sugar
170 g plain flour
Pinch of salt
1 teaspoon bicarbonate of soda
2 teaspoons ground ginger
1 teaspoon mixed spice
340 g medium oatmeal

Square (25 x 25 cm) cake tin, greased with butter and lined with baking parchment

1. Preheat the oven to 160°C/Gas Mark 3.
2. Put the treacle and butter in a large pan and heat gently until the butter has melted. Add the milk and sugar and heat until the sugar dissolves, stirring occasionally.
3. Sift the flour, salt, bicarbonate of soda, ground ginger and mixed spice into a large mixing bowl, and stir in the oatmeal.
4. Pour the liquid mix over the dry ingredients and mix thoroughly. Pour into the cake tin.
5. Bake for 50–60 minutes until the top is firm but not too dry. Good parkin errs on the side of moistness rather than dryness.
6. Leave the parkin in its tin on a wire rack to cool, then turn out and wrap in foil or greaseproof paper. Store in a tin for a few days before eating.

ROYAL (WRITING) ICING

Buns loom large in E. Nesbit's books where they are the stuff of treats and celebrations. No need for fancy pastries or posh gateaux; buns from the bakery are all that's needed to make an occasion special.

Whenever Mother in *The Railway Children* sells a story or a poem (that is, when an editor has been "sensible", as E. Nesbit notes pointedly), the children celebrate with "three‑pennyworth of halfpennies for tea". I enjoy the fact that they value these plain buns way beyond their actual cost because they mean so much to them in their temporary poverty. So we know that when they decide to forgo their next batch of buns in order to buy them for Perks on his birthday, the children are making a very generous sacrifice.

To make the fourteen birthday buns even more special Mother, in a very writerly fashion, decorates each one with Perks' initials, AP, using pink icing. At this point E. Nesbit breaks off to address the reader directly and to provide a delightfully detailed description of how this is achieved:

"You know how it's done, of course? You beat up whites of eggs and mix powdered sugar with them, and put in a few drops of cochineal. And then you make a cone of clean white paper with a lit‑tle hole at the pointed end, and put the pink egg-sugar in at the big end. It runs slowly out at the pointed end, and you write the letters with it just as though it were a great fat pen full of pink sugar-ink."

What a wonderful image. I'm sure this would make any reader want to reach for the nearest piping bag and begin their own writing career with icing and sponge instead of pen and paper.

When I was growing up you could ice anything in any colour – as long as it was pink. Cochineal was the only food colouring available in grocers' shops, so my reper- toire of icing went from the palest pink to the brightest carmine I could muster from the little bottle of finger-staining liquid. When I later discovered that cochineal is made from the dried and crushed bodies of the cochineal insect which lives on cacti in places like Lanzarote and Peru, it made my monochrome icing adventures suddenly appear rather more extravagant and exotic.

But these days cochineal isn't to be found in bottles, so you need to use red liquid colouring or, even better, a concentrated pink or red food-colouring paste (see Resources, page 297). And once you discover the joys of writing with icing, there's nothing to stop you using any colour that takes your fancy.

E. Nesbit's directions will stand you in good stead, or you can follow this more modern recipe which uses Merriwhite, an albumen substitute, instead of fresh egg whites. The icing in question is royal icing and is used for decorating and piping. It can be used to cover cakes, but because it sets hard and doesn't taste particularly nice, I recommend it's used just for the fancy bits, like initials and swirls and patterns and letters. See Pauline's Iced and Patterned Cakes (page 123) for basic cake icing that can be used as the writing surface. The cakes themselves can be iced with plain icing and then decorated with patterns using royal icing. Alternatively, use the recipe for Smashing Match Tea Jammy Buns (page 131) and ice the buns when they are completely cool, omitting the icing sugar on top and the fillings inside.

MAKES ENOUGH ICING TO WRITE ON SEVERAL DOZEN BUNS
1 tablespoon Merriwhite
500 g icing sugar
Red or pink food-colouring paste (optional)

Piping bag and fine nozzle (such as PME size 1); or a home-made paper piping bag or shop-bought reusable plastic piping bag

1. Place 1 tablespoon of the Merriwhite and 5 tablespoons of the icing sugar in a large bowl. Stir together.
2. Sieve in 100 g of the icing sugar and mix to a smooth paste. Continue to add the icing sugar in small quantities, beating all the time to ensure the mixture is smooth. An electric mixer or hand-held whisk will do the job best, although you can do it by hand. Add all the sugar in this way and beat until smooth and glossy. If you are colouring the icing, add your paste sparingly towards the end of adding the icing sugar so that you get the desired intensity of colour.
3. Cover tightly with clingfilm and leave to settle for a couple of hours or overnight.
4. When you are ready to ice, beat the icing well with a spoon to disperse the air bubbles that will have formed, then check its consistency. For writing and dots you need soft peaks – that is, when you draw your knife through the icing and pull it away a peak will form and the top will fall over. You may need to add a small amount of icing sugar to stiffen the icing or a drop of two of water to soften it. Fill the icing bags and start piping.

A RECIPE FOR DISASTER

O ne of the most thrilling aspects of children's literature is reading or listening to stories of badly behaved children. I don't mean wilfully or maliciously naughty children whose exploits are recounted in Victorian books in order to act as dreadful warnings, but children whose 'bad' behaviour stems from their willingness to follow their instinct and impulse rather than the codes set down by adults.

These children are the hungry ones. They have an equal hunger for food and for life. Since they often ignore or reject grown-ups' expectations they are wonderfully uninhibited, and their exploits are immensely exciting to well-behaved, conformist children who would love, just once, to behave the same way.

Pippi Longstocking is a heroine to many and her wild behaviour is the stuff of fantasy. How many children, after reading the Pippi books, have wanted to live on their own in a cottage in an orchard in Sweden and eat peppermints whenever they feel like it, bake pancakes (see Pippi's Swedish Pancakes, page 110) and heart-shaped ginger snaps (see Pippi Longstocking's Heart-Shaped Swedish Ginger Snaps, page 246) on a whim, play tag with policemen, and eat buns and drink tea in trees? She is exuberant, irrepressible and shockingly independent – not only do the adults in the village disapprove of her, so too did many parents when the book was first published in 1945.

So a genteel tea party at the house of her well-behaved friends, Tommy and Annika, is bound to be a test for Pippi. And she rises to the occasion magnificently. From her red chalk make-up and nail varnish, to her startling entrance, to her rush to pile her plate with cakes, add five lumps of sugar to her tea and then cram the dunked cakes whole into her mouth, she is dangerously, shockingly funny.

But there is more, for Astrid Lindgren realises that when it comes to food stories, children love a clownish carnival feast, complete with cream pies in the face. In the middle of the party, oblivious to the ladies' mounting disapproval, Pippi suddenly swoops down on to the large, centrepiece cream cake and removes the red sweet from the top with her teeth.

"But she had bent down a little too quickly and straightened up, her whole face was covered with cream.

'Ha ha ha,' laughed Pippi. 'Now we can play blind-man's-buff... I can't see a thing!'

Then she stuck out her tongue and licked off all the cream.

'Well, that was really quite an accident,' she said. 'But now the cake is just going to waste, so I might as well eat the whole thing.'

And she did."

Just rereading this now made me laugh out loud and reminded me how grateful I am for writers such as Astrid Lindgren who create exuberant, irrepressible, lovable characters whose zest and appetite for life is closely matched by that for large cream cakes. It may not be the best example of how to behave when having afternoon tea at Claridge's or The Ritz, but I would rather hear about Pippi and her enormous, Rabelaisian capacity for enjoyment than any number of stories designed to 'improve' my manners. And I know I am not alone.

A centrepiece Pippi-style cream cake for a genteel party should look like the kind of creamy confection that a clown might throw in the circus (complete with a red strawberry or cherry in the middle, rather like a clown's nose). This recipe fulfils the brief and makes a version of the traditional Swedish three-layer cake, which is filled with strawberries, covered with cream and enjoyed on Midsummer's Day. Different fruits or a mix of fruits work equally well. Raspberries, peaches, nectarines and cherries would all be delicious.

MAKES 1 LARGE CAKE (SERVES 8–10)

380 g caster sugar

230 g soft butter

4 eggs

250 ml buttermilk

1 teaspoon vanilla extract

Finely grated zest of 1 lemon
(unwaxed)

425 g self-raising flour

¼ teaspoon baking powder

¼ teaspoon bicarbonate of soda

750 ml cream

500 g strawberries

1 red sweet (optional)

24-cm round cake or spring-form tin, greased with butter and lined with baking parchment

1. Preheat the oven to 180°C/Gas Mark 4.
2. In a large mixing bowl, cream the sugar and butter together until pale and fluffy.
3. Beat in the eggs one at a time.
4. Add the buttermilk, vanilla extract and lemon zest and stir to mix. Sift in the flour, baking powder and bicarbonate of soda and fold in gently with a large metal spoon until all the ingredients are just combined.
5. Spoon the mix into the tin and bake for 55–60 minutes until the cake is well risen and a metal skewer or sharp knife inserted in it comes out clean.
6. Leave the cake in its tin on a wire rack to cool completely, then turn out.
7. Cut the cake in half horizontally with a sharp knife. Whip the cream and spread about a third on the bottom layer. Reserve one good strawberry and scatter the remaining ones on top of the cream. Gently replace the top layer of sponge.
8. Spread the remaining cream generously over the top and sides of the cake, and place the single strawberry (or a red sweet if you prefer) in the centre.
9. Serve immediately.

BAD HARRY'S
BIRTHDAY TRIFLE

There is an exquisite delight mingled with pain that comes as you read or listen to stories and you *know* without a shadow of a doubt that the main character is going to be naughty. I was the archetypal Sensible Big Sister so I adored *My Naughty Little Sister* by Dorothy Edwards and could never get enough of the heroine's naughtiness, but I also knew that underneath the apparently wilfully naughty exterior was a very sweet, natural, curious little girl.

I can still recall the terrified tummy-turning that accompanied my favourite story of all, 'My Naughty Little Sister at the party'. She and her partner in crime, Bad Harry, absent themselves from his birthday party at which all the nice little children are playing party games, admire the party tea in the next room, then sneak into the larder where the pièce de résistance, a surprise treat, is hidden.

"… Bad Harry showed my naughty little sister a lovely spongy trifle, covered with creamy stuff and with silver balls and jelly-sweets on the top. And my naughty little sister stared more than ever because the liked spongy trifle better than jellies or blancmanges or biscuits or sandwiches or cakes-with-cherries-on, or even birthday-cake, so she said, 'For me.'

Bad Harry said, 'For me too.'"

And it is inevitable that they are going to pick off a sweet and a ball, then go deeper and deeper until the whole thing is so "untidy" that they eat almost the entire trifle, and are only prevented from doing so by the arrival of Bad Harry's mother.

The naughty little sister's punishment is a bad night's sleep and a life-long aversion to spongy trifle, but the reader understands that she has had an experience that

many children would repeat, given half the chance and a little more privacy in the larder.

My Naughty Little Sister stories have all the flavour of the 1950s. This was a decade of gaudy, elaborate and excessively decorated food, and trifles with layers of vivid colour and sparkly, sugary, unnatural toppings were made by every chic hostess. I know the trifle has moved on since then but, in the interests of authenticity, and so that you can recreate a taste of the 1950s, here are two recipes for classic, iconic, multicoloured trifles. One contains alcohol and one contains jelly, but there is nothing to stop you mixing and matching the layers to suit your preference and guests.

Before making either recipe, first choose your best trifle bowl; the whole point of trifle is that you should be able to see and appreciate the layers through the sides of a glass bowl. It should be large and have a relatively flat base.

TIPSY TRIFLE

MAKES 1 LARGE TRIFLE (SERVES 6–8)

6–8 trifle sponges (enough to cover the base of your trifle bowl)
Raspberry jam
100 ml sweet sherry, Madeira or Marsala
2 tins raspberries in fruit juice
600 ml custard, made with custard powder
1 x 284 ml carton double cream
Silver balls, hundreds and thousands, glacé cherries or angelica, to decorate

1. Slice each trifle sponge open horizontally and spread one side with raspberry jam. Place the tops back on and arrange on the bottom of the bowl. Pour your chosen alcohol evenly over the sponges. Leave to soak for 5 minutes while you deal with the raspberries and make the custard.

2. Drain the liquid from the tinned raspberries and scatter the fruit on top of the sponges.

3. Make the custard according to the instructions on the tin. Pour this over the sponges and raspberries and leave until cold. It's best to set the trifle aside at this point for a few hours or overnight so that the flavours develop fully.

4. When you are ready to serve the trifle, whisk the cream until soft peaks form, and spoon it over the custard.

5. You should now have a wonderful, stripy trifle with a snowy white surface, which you can decorate as you please, using silver balls, hundreds and thousands, glacé cherries or pieces of angelica.

6. Stand back, admire, and serve before anyone starts digging into the bowl uninvited.

JELLY TRIFLE

MAKES 1 LARGE TRIFLE (SERVES 6–8)

6–8 trifle sponges or trifle sponge fingers (enough to cover the base of your trifle bowl)
2 tins of raspberries in fruit juice
1 packet raspberry jelly
600 ml custard, made with custard powder
1 x 284 ml carton double cream
Silver balls, hundreds and thousands, cherries or angelica, to decorate

1. Cover the base of your trifle bowl with the trifle sponges or trifle sponge fingers.
2. Drain the liquid from the tinned raspberries and scatter the fruit on top of the sponges.
3. Make up the jelly with 450 ml water (instead of the usual 600 ml), and carefully this pour over the sponges and raspberries. Leave to set completely before making the next layer.
4. When the jelly has set, make the custard according to the instructions on the tin. Allow it to cool a little (otherwise it will melt the jelly below) then pour it over the jelly and leave until cold.
5. When you are ready to serve the trifle, whisk the double cream until soft peaks form, and spoon it over the custard.

See Steps 5 and 6 of Tipsy Trifle.

SUGAR ON SNOW

When I was eleven I had to memorise the poem 'Silver' by Walter de la Mare for an exam. I have never forgotten its opening lines: 'Slowly, silently, now the moon, walks the night in her silver shoon', with all those soft, sibilant sounds that are so magical and evocative. The appeal of 'sugar on snow', the more popular and poetic name for maple syrup candy, works on the same principle, I think, because there is something similarly wondrous about the simplicity and purity of the sounds, as well as the idea of drizzling a thin stream of hot syrup on to fresh, white snow and eating it immediately after it has been transformed into a chewy treat.

Not that Laura Ingalls Wilder calls it 'sugar on snow' in *The Little House in the Big Woods* – but when Grandma makes maple syrup candy, we have one of the most memorable food moments in children's literature. The very special "sugar snow" creates the ideal conditions for collecting maple sap to make syrup, and family and friends are all conscripted to help; and celebrate later with a big party at which the highlight is maple syrup candy.

Grandma boils up the syrup until it "waxes" and then, with a big wooden spoon, she pours hot syrup on to each person's plate of freshly gathered snow. In an instant it cools into candy which is eaten as fast as possible by everyone, young and old, at the party. It's all wonderful, family, snowy fun and I think it could be a great way of enjoying the rare, special times when snow falls in Britain.

And should there ever be a really deep, thick blanket of snow, I'll be tempted to take the pan outside and fling the syrup directly on to it, and make wild patterns and swirls on the huge, blank, white canvas in a grand Jackson Pollock style.

This treat can be created quite easily in the absence of snow, although pouring the hot syrup on to crushed ice may not feel quite as poetic flinging it over a layer of glistening, crystalline snow. Nevertheless, it's enjoyable to make, especially if you use wooden lollipop sticks to roll up the strands of sticky candy.

For a traditional and authentic sugar snow party, serve the candy with coffee, beer, doughnuts, sour pickles (gherkins) and saltines (salted crackers).

MAKES ENOUGH FOR 4–6 PEOPLE TO PLAY
500 ml maple syrup
Clean snow or crushed ice

1. Gather the snow on large plates (one per person) and leave outside by the back door. If you are using crushed ice, have your plateful(s) at the ready in the freezer.
2. Boil the syrup to 124°C or hard crack stage on a sugar thermometer. This will take about 6–7 minutes. If you don't have a sugar thermometer, test by dropping a small amount of the syrup into a small bowl of iced water. If the syrup forms long threads that are pliable (not breakable), the correct temperature has been reached.
3. Allow the syrup to cool for a couple of minutes so that the boiling subsides.
4. Bring in the plates from outside or retrieve from the freezer. If you are going for the Jackson Pollock effect, take the pan of syrup outside.
5. With a wooden or metal spoon, quickly drizzle strips, lines, squiggles, doodles, letters, lattices, lace, messages on to the surface of the snow or ice. Don't drop large dollops of syrup because they will melt the snow and fall through. The syrup will be transformed on contact with the snow into a waxy, chewy candy.
6. Make maple syrup lollipops by quickly running a wooden stick along a strip and twirling it; the candy will roll up into a lolly.

$\mathscr{A}$ND $\mathscr{A}$FTERWARDS ...

$\mathbf{A}$while ago, there was a media craze for looking through famous people's rubbish in order to piece together intimate details of their lives and lifestyles. The findings of these scavenging intrusions never interested me unless they contained food, because that I *do* find revealing and fascinating.

So I am riveted by the food that Wilbur the pig eats in E.B. White's *Charlotte's Web* (1952), consisting as it does of all the leftovers from the Zuckermans' kitchen. The carefully constructed lists reveal a classic, mid-twentieth-century, East Coast American home-cooked diet that is amazing in its variety and abundance. In it we find all the staples of what is fast becoming nostalgia food: food from an apparently bygone era which is, in fact, only fifty years ago.

It is also amuses me that Wilbur's diet contains the kind of strange, appealing mix of foodstuffs that many children, as well as a well-loved pig, would happily eat. It includes "bits of doughnuts, wheat cakes with drops of maple syrup sticking to them, left-over custard pudding with raisins, apple parings, fried potatoes, marmalade drippings, a piece of baked apple, a scrap of upside-down cake, left-over pancakes, a third of a ginger snap, the skin off a cup of cocoa, an ancient jelly roll, and a spoon-ful of raspberry jelly."

If you look more closely, you will see that E.B. White also includes scraps of meat, fruit, grains, cheese and fish so that Wilbur enjoys a perfectly balanced diet, one that is far better than that of most humans nowadays.

All this makes me wonder whether perhaps we should review what we throw away a little more carefully in the light of what we eat in the first place. If we take the trouble to shop carefully, make our own treats and eat simple, fresh foods, the kind that recur time and again in the recipes and food included in this book, then we shouldn't have to fill our bins with leftovers. Unless, of course, we have a pig to feed and keep happy.

ACKNOWLEDGEMENTS

I am grateful to all the publishers and copyright holders who have kindly granted permission to quote from some of the world's best-loved children's books and to use the marvellous illustrations that grace the pages of this book.

I consider myself extremely fortunate to work with such an outstanding publisher, and I would like thank the team at Hodder & Stoughton for making this book a reality. In particular my editor, Nicky Ross, deserves a huge vote of thanks for taking over so calmly and seamlessly from Sarah Reece. I am also indebted to Hannah Knowles and Tessa Clark for their help with the huge task of permissions, and grateful thanks to Sarah Hammond for her excellent management of the complex process of bringing the book's various elements together.

I would also like to express my gratitude to Jane Graham Maw and Jennifer Christie of Graham Maw Christie who have once again been unfailingly helpful, encouraging and good-humoured agents.

Selecting the books to include here was no easy task but I was helped enormously by several people. My early reading supplied a solid basis on which to build; as a child I was fortunate to have complete literary freedom and plenty of library tickets, plus the unwavering support and encouragement of my mum, Sheila Mills. Thanks, Mum.

The readers of my blog, yarnstorm, were also extremely helpful and I am grateful to everyone who left comments or emailed me with suggestions. I would especially like to thank Irene Vandervoort in New York. When it came to American literature, Irene's assitance was invaluable; she very kindly answered my queries, sent me books and supplied me with an excellent list of American children's classics. And from the very outset Angela Burdett has been wonderfully enthusiastic and supportive, and I owe her many thanks for being a great listener and questioner.

Then there is my family, the people at home who have lived with this project – the books, the baking, the writing – from start to finish. I want to thank my husband Simon for believing in the original idea and for pushing me for several years to get the book written, for dealing manfully with the huge quantities of baked goods that appeared in the kitchen during recipe-testing, for never complaining about the piles of books everywhere, and for being the best.

Most of all, I want to thank my children, Phoebe, Alice and Tom. It was through the experience of reading to them day after day, night after night, year after year, that I had the joy of rediscovering many marvellous children's books in their company. Thank you for always being ready to enjoy a good story.

There is one person, though, who deserves a very special thank you, and that is Phoebe. Phoebe helped me from the very moment of this book's conception and proved to be an amazing literary and culinary assistant. She trawled through masses of books for food references, pored over cookery books, spent hours in the kitchen testing recipes with me, and offered invaluable feedback and suggestions. It has been a privilege and a delight to work with her.

Hodder & Stoughton would like to thank the following for permission to reproduce illustrations and copyright material in this book.

Every reasonable effort has been made to contact the copyright holders, but if there are any errors or omissions, Hodder & Stoughton will be pleased to insert the appropriate acknowledgement in any subsequent printing of this publication.

Text Acknowledgements

Enid Blyton, *The Adventurous Four* © 1941 Chorion Rights Limited. All rights reserved; Enid Blyton, *The Circus of Adventure*, Enid Blyton (Macmillan Children's Books, 2005). Reproduced by permission of Macmillan Children's Books UK; Enid Blyton, *Five Go Down to the Sea* © 1953 Chorion Rights Limited. All rights reserved; Enid Blyton, *Five Go on Kirrin Island Again* © 1947 Chorion Rights Limited. All rights reserved; Enid Blyton, *Five on a Treasure Island* © 1942 Chorion Rights Limited. All rights reserved; Enid Blyton, *Five on Finniston Farm* © 1960 Chorion Rights Limited. All rights reserved; Enid Blyton, *Five Run Away Together* © 1944 Chorion Rights Limited. All rights reserved; Enid Blyton, *The Folk of the Faraway Tree* © 1946 Chorion Rights Limited. All rights reserved; Enid Blyton, *In the Fifth at Malory Towers* © 1950 Chorion Rights Limited. All rights reserved; Enid Blyton, *The O'Sullivan Twins* © 1942 Chorion Rights Limited. All rights reserved; Enid Blyton, *The Ragamuffin Mystery* © 1959 Chorion Rights Limited. All rights reserved; Enid Blyton, *The Rilloby Fair Mystery* © 1950 Chorion Rights Limited. All rights reserved; Enid Blyton, *The Rubadub Mystery* © 1952 Chorion Rights Limited. All rights reserved; Enid Blyton, *The Rocking-down Mystery* © 1952 Chorion Rights Limited. All rights reserved; Enid Blyton, *The Rat-a-Tat Mystery* © 1956 Chorion Rights Limited. All rights reserved; Enid Blyton, *The Second Form at St Clare's* © 1944 Chorion Rights Limited. All rights reserved; Enid Blyton, *The Secret of Spiggy Holes*, Basil Blackwell (1940); Enid Blyton, *Secret Seven Win Through* © 1955 Chorion Rights Limited. All rights reserved; Enid Blyton, *Upper Fourth at Malory Towers* © 1949 Chorion Rights Limited. All rights reserved; Elinor M. Brent-Dyer, *The School at the Chalet*, quoted by permission of Girls Gone By Publishers; Joyce Lankester Brisley, *The Adventures of Milly-Molly-Mandy*, (Puffin, 1992). Reproduced by permission of

Delights. Reproduced by permission of The Society of Authors as the literary representative of the Estate of John Masefield; Mary Norton *The Borrowers* (Puffin). Reproduced by permission of Orion Children's Books; Philippa Pearce, *Tom's Midnight Garden*, Puffin (1993). Reproduced by permission of Oxford University Press; Arthur Ransome, *Swallows and Amazons/Swallowdale*. Published by Jonathan Cape. Reprinted by permission of The Random House Group; Johanna Spyri, *Heidi*. Published by Dell Yearling (1990). Used with permission; Noel Streatfeild, *Ballet Shoes*, (Puffin). Reproduced by permission of Orion Children's Books; Noel Streatfeild, *Dancing Shoes*, Hodder and Stoughton Ltd, copyright © 1995. Reproduced by permission of Hodder and Stoughton Ltd; P.L. Travers, *Mary Poppins*, copyright 1934 and renewed 1962, reprinted by permission of Houghton Mifflin Harcourt Publishing Company and the trustees of the P.L. Travers Will Trust; P.L. Travers, *Mary Poppins Comes Back*, copyright 1935 and renewed 1963, reprinted by permission of Harcourt, Inc. and the trustees of the P L Travers Will Trust; Ethel Turner, *Seven Little Australians* (Ward Lock & Co. London and Melbourne, 1941). Reproduced with permission by Penguin Group (Australia); E.B. White, *Charlotte's Web* (Hamish Hamilton, 1952) Copyright © 1952 by J. White.

PICTURE ACKNOWLEDGEMENTS

Enid Blyton, *Five Go Off in a Caravan* © 1997. Illustration by Eileen A. Soper, reproduced by permission of Hodder & Stoughton Ltd: 9, 53; Enid Blyton, *Five on a Treasure Island* © 1997. Illustration by Eileen A. Soper, reproduced by permission of Hodder & Stoughton Ltd: 67, 173; Enid Blyton, *Five on Kirrin Island Again* © 1997. Illustration by Eileen A. Soper, reproduced by permission of Hodder & Stoughton Ltd: 109; Enid Blyton, *Five Run Away Together* © 1997. Illustration by Eileen A. Soper, reproduced by permission of Hodder & Stoughton Ltd:

148, 157, 194; Enid Blyton, *The Folk of the Faraway Tree*, illustration by Dorothy M. Wheeler, published by George Newnes Ltd: vii, 191; Enid Blyton, *The O'Sullivan Twins*, illustration by W. Lindsay Cable, published by Methuen: 266; Enid Blyton, *The Rat-a-Tat Mystery*, illustration by Anyon Cook, published by Collins: 6; Enid Blyton, *The Rub-a-Dub Mystery*, illustration by Gilbert Dunlop, published by Collins: 197, 178; Enid Blyton, *The Secret of Spiggy Holes*, illustration by E.H. Davie, published by Basil Blackwell, used with kind permission: 6, 25, 115, 129, 125, 145, 165, 169, 224, 293; Enid Blyton, *The Secret Seven* © 1996. Illustration by George Brook, reproduced by permission of Hodder & Stoughton Ltd: 240; Enid Blyton, *The Treasure Hunters*, illustration by Barbara Freeman, published by Collins: 15, 30; Edward Bond, *A Bear Called Paddington* © 2003. Illustration by Peggy Fortnum, reprinted by permission of HarperCollins Publishers Ltd: 37; Joyce Lankester Brisley, *The Adventures of Milly-Molly-Mandy*, reproduced by permission of Macmillan Children's Books UK: 1, 13, 57, 79, 81, 117, 152, 235; Frances Hodgson Burnett, *The Secret Garden*, illustration by Robin Lawrie, published by Puffin. Used by kind permission: 253; Frances Coolidge, *What Katy Did*, illustration by Neil Reed, published by Puffin. Used by kind permission: 243; Richmal Crompton, *Just William*, reproduced by permission of Macmillan Children's Books UK: 209; Roald Dahl, *Matilda*, illustration by Quentin Blake, published by Jonathan Cape. Reprinted by permission of The Random House Group Ltd.: 249; Dorothy Edwards, *My Naughty Little Sister*, illustration by Shirley Hughes, published by Egmont. Used by kind permission: 279; Elizabeth Goudge, *Linnets and Valerians*, illustration by Ian Ribbons, published by Hodder & Stoughton: 127; Kenneth Grahame, *The Wind in the Willows*, copyright © The Estate of E.H. Shepard reproduced with permission of Curtis Brown Limited, London: 176; Laura Ingalls Wilder, *Little House in the Big Woods*, published by Egmont: 282; Laura Ingalls Wilder, *Little House on the Prairie*, published by Egmont: 112; C.S. Lewis, The Lion, the Witch and the Wardrobe, copyright © C.S. Lewis Pte. Ltd. 1950. Illustrations by Pauline Baynes copyright © C.S. Lewis Pte. Ltd. 1950. Reprinted by permission: 53, 61; E. Nesbit, A Little Princess, illustration by Marjory Gill, published by Puffin: 226; E. Nesbit, Five Children and It, illustration by H.R. Millar, published by Puffin: 89; E. Nesbit, The Railway Children, illustration by C.E. Brooks, published by Puffin: 272; Mary Norton, The Borrowers, illustration by Sian Bailey, published by Puffin: 43; Arthur Ransome, Swallows and Amazons, published by Jonathan Cape. Reprinted by permission of The Random House Group Ltd: 151, 161; Johanna Spyri, Heidi, illustration by Cecil Edwards, published by Puffin: 82; Noel Streatfeild, Ballet Shoes, illustration by Ruth Gervis, reproduced by permission of Orion Children's Books: 125; P.L. Travers, Mary Poppins, illustration by Mary Shepard, reprinted by permission of HarperCollins Publishers Ltd: 199, 267; E.B. White, Charlotte's Web, illustration by Garth Williams, published by Puffin: 285.

*B*IBLIOGRAPHY

CHILDREN'S BOOKS

This is the list of the books I refer to in the text with the details of the editions in which I read them. All but a handful are still in print. Most are available in more up-to-date editions in shops and on book websites such as www.amazon.co.uk (www.amazon.com in the US).

Second-hand bookshops are a great source of children's books if you are not too fussy about the date of publication. Alternatively, I use two excellent websites for used books: www.abebooks.co.uk (www.abebooks.com in the US) and www.alibris.co.uk (www.alibris.com in the US).

Little Women, Louisa May Alcott (Puffin, 2003)

By Enid Blyton
  The Circus of Adventure (Macmillan Children's Books, 2002)
  The Folk of the Faraway Tree (George Newnes, 1946)
  Mr Galliano's Circus (Armada, 1962)

The Secret of Spiggy Holes (Basil Blackwell, 1940)
The Treasure Hunters (Collins, 1966)

Famous Five series
(Hodder Children's Books, 1997)
Secret Seven series
(Hodder Children's Books, 1996)
The Five Find-Outer series (Egmont, 2003)

The Barney 'R' Mysteries:
The Rockingdown Mystery (Collins, 1961)
The Rilloby Fair Mystery (Collins, 1964)
The Ring O'Bells Mystery (Collins, 1951)
The Rubadub Mystery (Collins, 1952)
The Rat-A-Tat Mystery (Collins, 1956)
The Ragamuffin Mystery (Collins, 1959)

Malory Towers series
First Term at Malory Towers (Methuen, 1946)
Second Form at Malory Towers (Methuen, 1947)
Third Year at Malory Towers (Dragon Books, 1975)
Upper Fourth at Malory Towers (Methuen, 1949)
In the Fifth at Malory Towers (Dragon Books, 1974)

The Twins at St Clare's series
The Twins at St Clare's (Egmont, 2000)
The O'Sullivan Twins (Egmont, 2000)
The Second Form at St Clare's (Egmont, 2000)

A Bear Called Paddington Michael Bond (Collins, 2003)

The Swish of the Curtain Pamela Brown (T. Nelson, 1941)

The School at the Chalet Elinor M Brent-Dyer (W&R Chambers, 1925)

Jennings Goes to School Anthony Buckeridge (Puffin, 1965)

What Katy Did Susan Coolidge (Puffin,1995)

What Katy Did At School Susan Coolidge (Puffin, 1994)

Just William Richmal Crompton (Macmillan Children's Books, 2005)

Matilda Roald Dahl (Puffin, 2007)

My Naughty Little Sister Dorothy Edwards (Egmont, 2002)

Chitty Chitty Bang Bang Ian Fleming (Puffin, 2001)

The Family From One End Street Eve Garnett (Puffin, 1994)

The Little White Horse Elizabeth Goudge (Lion Hudson, 2000)

Linnets and Valerians Elizabeth Goudge (Knight Books, 1982)

Henrietta's House Elizabeth Goudge (University of London Press, 1946)

The Wind in the Willows Kenneth Grahame (Egmont, 2000)

A Little Bushmaid Mary Grant Bruce (Ward, Lock & Co., 1910)

Mates at Billabong Mary Grant Bruce (Ward, Lock & Co., 1911)

Back to Billabong Mary Grant Bruce (Ward, Lock & Co., 1921)

The Secret Garden Frances Hodgson Burnett (Puffin, 1994)

A Little Princess Frances Hodgson Burnett (Puffin, 2003)

Little House on the Prairie Laura Ingalls Wilder (Egmont, 2000)

Little House in the Big Woods Laura Ingalls Wilder (Egmont, 2000)

The Adventures of Milly-Molly-Mandy (four collections of stories) Joyce
  Lankester Brisley (Puffin, 1992)

The Lion, the Witch and the Wardrobe C.S. Lewis (Collins, 2001)

Pippi Longstocking Astrid Lindgren (Oxford University Press, 2004)

The Box of Delights John Masefield (Egmont, 2000)

Anne of Green Gables L.M. Montgomery (Puffin, 1994)

Five Children and It E. Nesbit (Puffins 2004)

The Railway Children E. Nesbit (Puffin, 2003)

The Phoenix and the Carpet E. Nesbit (Puffin, 2004)

The Story of the Treasure Seekers E. Nesbit (Puffin, 1994)

The Borrowers Mary Norton (Puffin, 2003)

Tom's Midnight Garden Philippa Pearce (Puffin, 2003)

Pollyanna Eleanor H Porter (Puffin, 2003)

Swallows and Amazons Arthur Ransome (Red Fox, 2001)

Swallowdale Arthur Ransome (Red Fox, 2001)

Billy Bunter of Greyfriars School Frank Richards (Charles Skilton, 1947)

Heidi Johanna Spyri (Puffin, 2003)

Dancing Shoes Noel Streatfeild (Hodder Children's Books, 1995)

Ballet Shoes Noel Streatfeild (Puffin, 2004)

Mary Poppins P.L. Travers (Collins, 1998)

Mary Poppins Comes Back P.L. Travers (Harcourt, 1997)

Seven Little Australians Ethel Turner (Ward, Lock & Co, 1941)

Molesworth Geoffrey Willans & Ronald Searle (Penguin, 2000)

Daddy-Long-Legs Jean Webster (Puffin, 1995)

Charlotte's Web E.B. White (Puffin, 1993)

COOKERY BOOKS

Some of the titles in the following list are out of out of print, but can be tracked down on www.abebooks.co.uk (or www.abebooks.com in the US). I also use www.alibris.co.uk (www.alibris.com in the US) for second-hand books.

For the best selection of cookery books under one roof, I recommend Books for Cooks.

Books for Cooks
4 Blenheim Crescent
London W11 1NN
Tel: 020 7221 1992
www.booksforcooks.com

Talking About Cakes Margaret Bates (Penguin, 1977)

Delia Smith's Book of Cakes Delia Smith (Coronet, 1988)

The Fannie Farmer Baking Book Marion Cunningham (Alfred A. Knopf, 1984)

The Breakfast Book Marion Cunningham (Alfred A. Knopf, 1990)

How to Eat Nigella Lawson (Chatto & Windus, 1998)

How to be a Domestic Goddess Nigella Lawson (Chatto & Windus, 2000)

Nigel Slater's Real Food Nigel Slater (Fourth Estate, 1998)

Appetite Nigel Slater (Fourth Estate, 2000)

The Kitchen Diaries Nigel Slater (Fourth Estate, 2005)

The Bread Book Linda Collister and Anthony Blake (Conran Octopus, 1993)

The Baking Book Linda Collister and Anthony Blake (Conran Octopus, 1996)

Baker & Spice Baking with Passion Dan Lepard and Richard Whittington

(Quadrille, 1999)

Cakes Barbara Maher (Penguin, 1984)

Good Things in England Florence White (Persephone, 1999)

Kitchen Essays Agnes Jekyll (Persephone, 2001)

English Food Jane Grigson (Penguin, 1993)

Simply British Sybil Kapoor (Penguin, 1998)

Food in England Dorothy Hartley (Little, Brown, 1999)

Beeton's Book of Household Management ed. Mrs Isabella Beeton (S.O. Beeton, 1863)

Margaret Costa's Four Seasons Cookery Book Margaret Costa (Grub Street, 1996)

English Bread and Yeast Cookery Elizabeth David (Penguin, 1979)

The Swedish Table Helene Henderson (University of Minnesota Press, 2005)

RESOURCES

LONDON

Jane Asher Party Cakes and Sugarcraft
22–24 Cale Street
London SW3 3QU
Tel: 020 7584 6177
www.jane-asher.co.uk

Huge range of high-quality baking and decorating equipment. Also sells Sugarflair food-colouring paste and everything you need for icing cakes.

SURREY

Squires
Squires House
3 Waverley Lane
Farnham GU9 8BB
Surrey
Tel: 0845 2255671
www.squires-group.co.uk

On-line shopping at: www.squires-shop.com
    Supplier of the excellent Squires food-colouring paste. Also great for baking tins, bun and muffins cases, cake decorations and equipment.

Nationwide

John Lewis

See website for branch locations. John Lewis also offers an excellent on-line shopping service:

www.johnlewis.com

While it may not have fancy food colours and cake decorations, John Lewis does stock just about everything else you need for baking. I buy all my basics here: tins, knives, bowls, whisks, pastry brushes, oven gloves, and the old-fashioned cream-and biscuit-coloured Mason Cash mixing bowls.

Waitrose

www.waitrose.com

The best supermarket for high-quality baking ingredients such as unbleached organic flours, vanilla extract, various sugars, butters and dried fruits.

De Cuisine

www.decuisine.co.uk

Wonderful website for high-quality baking equipment.

Toasting forks

www.cookware-online.co.uk has some excellent stainless steel toasting forks.

INDEX

A

adventure 147–8
   recipes for the adventurous life
      147–67
The Adventures of Milly-Molly-
   Mandy (Joyce Lankester Brisley)
   78–9, 80–2
   Milly-Molly-Mandy Goes
      Sledging 117–18
   Milly-Molly-Mandy has Friends
      56–7
The Adventurous Four: Shipwrecked!
   (Enid Blyton) 171–3
Alcott, Louisa May: *Little Women*
   142, 237
Anne of Green Gables
   (L.M. Montgomery) 97–8, 115,
   120–1, 256
appetite 252–3
   see also hunger, recipe for

apple cake 136–8
apples 237–8

B

bacon with hash browns 18–19
baking 115–16
Ballet Shoes (Noel Streatfeild) 123,
   258–9
Barney 'R' Mysteries (Enid Blyton) 74
Baynes, Pauline 52
A Bear called Paddington (Michael
   Bond) 26
   Paddington's marmalade buns 37–9
Billabong stories (Mary Grant Bruce)
   40–1, 43
biscuits
   ginger 107–8, 246–8
   squashed fly 162–4
   sugar 230–2
Blyton, Enid 130, 171, 178, 180

The Adventurous Four: Shipwrecked! 171–3

Barney 'R' Mysteries 74

breakfasts 16

The Circus of Adventure 47–8

Famous Five series *see* Famous Five series

Five Find-Outer series 44, 205, 212, 260–1

The Folk of the Faraway Tree 190

Malory Towers series 69

Mr Galliano series 152

Naughtiest Girl stories 134

The Ragamuffin Mystery 10, 230

The Rilloby Fair Mystery 16, 233

The Rockingdown Mystery 72, 99

The Rubadub Mystery 74

The Secret of Spiggy Holes 166, 223–4

Secret Seven series 239

The Treasure Hunters 30–1

The Twins at St Clare's series 144–5, 205

Bond, Michael: *A Bear called Paddington* 26

Paddington's marmalade buns 37–9

The Borrowers (Mary Norton) 85

The Box of Delights (John Masefield) 92, 254

bread 27–9

cornbread 112–14

damper 182–4

Swiss cheese and bread supper 83–4

see also toast

breakfast 13–14

recipes for 16–24

Brent-Dyer, Elinor M. 130

Chalet School series 136

Brisley, Joyce Lankester: *The Adventures of Milly-Molly-Mandy* 56–7, 78–9, 80–2, 117–18

Brown, Pamela: *The Swish of the Curtain* 261

Bruce, Mary Grant: Billabong stories 40–1, 43

bunloaf 159–60

buns

currant 226–9

hot cross 33–6

jammy 131–3

marmalade 37–9

rock 239–41

Burnett, Frances Hodgson

A Little Princess 226–7

The Secret Garden 13, 174, 252–3

C

cake
  apple 136–8
  bunloaf 159–60
  cherry 64–5
  chocolate 249–51
  chocolate éclairs 205–7
  coconut 54–5
  cream 276–7
  fruit 69–73
  ginger 66–8
  gingerbread 202–4
  iced and patterned 123–5
  jumbles 105–6
  layer cake 120–2
  parkin 270–1
  patty-pan 117–18
  raspberry jam cakes 199–201
  royal icing 272–4
  saffron 102–4
  seed 154–5
  tinned pineapple 156–8

walnut 41–3
calf's-foot jelly 218–19
candy pull 139–41
Chalet School series (Elinor M. Brent-Dyer) 136
Charlotte's Web (E.B. White) 18, 285–6
cheese
  Swiss cheese and bread supper 83–4
  on toast 53
cherry cake 64–5
chicken soup 220
Chitty Chitty Bang Bang (Ian Fleming) 185–6
chocolate cake 249–51
chocolate éclairs 205–7
The Circus of Adventure (Enid Blyton) 47–8
cocoa 165–7
coconut cakes 54–5
coconut kisses 210–11
Coolidge, Susan: *What Katy Did* novels 97, 105–6, 134–5, 242–3
cordial, raspberry 256–7
cornbread 112–14
cream cake 276–7
cress sandwiches 176–7

Crompton, Richmal: *Just William*
    126, 210–11, 260
crumpets 267–9
currant buns 226–9

D

Daddy Long-Legs (Jean Webster)
    139, 142
Dahl, Roald: *Matilda* 249–51
damper 182–4
Dancing Shoes (Noel Streatfeild) 20, 33
de la Mare, Walter J. 282

E

éclairs 205–7
Edwardian larder 88–9
Edwards, Dorothy: *My Naughty Little
    Sister* 278–9
eggs
    boiled 20–1
    hard-boiled 171–3
    roasted 174–5
    scrambled 149–50

elevenses 25–6
    Melbourne morning tea 40–1
    recipes for 27–45
The Enchanted Castle (E. Nesbit)
    188–9

F

The Family from One End Street (Eve
    Garnett) 214, 260
Famous Five series (Enid Blyton) 153
    Five Go on Kirrin Island Again 107
    Five Go to Mystery Moor 64
    Five on a Treasure Island 66–7
    Five on Finniston Farm 44–5
    Five Run Away Together 27, 156, 193
Five Children and It (E. Nesbit) 260
Five Find-Outer series (Enid
    Blyton) 44, 205, 212, 260–1
Five Go on Kirrin Island Again
    (Enid Blyton) 107
Five Go to Mystery Moor (Enid Bly-
    ton) 64
Five on a Treasure Island (Enid Bly-
    ton) 66–7
Five on Finniston Farm (Enid Blyton)

44–5

Five Run Away Together (Enid Blyton) 27, 156, 193

Fleming, Ian: *Chitty Chitty Bang Bang* 185–6

The Folk of the Faraway Tree (Enid Blyton) 190

fruit

pickled 142–3

raw 178–9, 188–9, 237–8

stewed 49–51

see also specific fruits

fruit cake 69–71

'Diana's favourite fruity fruit cake' 72–3

G

Garnett, Eve: *The Family from One End Street* 214, 260

ghostbusting tea 76

ginger beer 193–5

ginger biscuits 107–8

ginger cake 66–8

ginger drink, hot 258–9

ginger snaps 246–8

gingerbread 202–4

going out treats 197–216

gooseberries ('goosegogs') 188–9

Goudge, Elizabeth

Henrietta's House 49–50

Linnets and Valerians 126–7, 208–9

The Little White Horse 14, 77, 97, 102, 217, 230, 270–1

Grahame, Kenneth: *The Wind in the Willows* 176

H

hash browns 18–19

Heidi (Johanna Spyri) 83

Henrietta's House (Elizabeth Goudge) 49–50

honey on toast 53

hot cross buns 33–6

hunger, recipe for 11

I

ice cream

dairy ices 212–13

sundaes 214–16
icing, royal 272–4
Ingalls Wilder, Laura: Little House
   stories 22, 97, 112–13, 282

J

jam
   jammy buns 131–3
   puffs 185–7
   raspberry jam cakes 199–201
   scones 223–5
   strawberry 126–8
   tarts 30–2
Jekyll, Agnes 105
jelly trifle 281
jumbles 105–6
junket 221–2
Just William (Richmal Crompton)
   126, 210–11, 260

L

Landers, Ann 18
Larkin, Philip 5

layer cake 120–2
leftovers 285–6
lemonade 190–2
Lepard, Dan 34
Lewis, C.S.: *The Lion, the Witch and
   the Wardrobe* 52–3, 60, 262
limes, pickled 142–3
Lindgren, Astrid: *Pippi Longstocking*
   110, 236, 246–7, 275–6
Linnets and Valerians (Elizabeth
   Goudge) 126–7, 208–9
*The Lion, the Witch and the
   Wardrobe* (C.S. Lewis) 52–3, 60,
   262
Little House in the Big Woods (Laura
   Ingalls Wilder) 22, 97, 282
Little House on the Prairie (Laura In-
   galls Wilder) 112–13
A Little Princess (Frances
   Hodgson Burnett) 226–7
The Little White Horse (Elizabeth
   Goudge) 14, 77, 97, 102, 217, 230,
   270–1
Little Women (Alcott, Louisa May)
   142, 237

M

macaroons 44–5
  coconut kisses 210–11
Malory Towers series (Enid Blyton)
  69
marmalade buns 37–9
marmalade roll 60–3
Mary Poppins (P.L. Travers)
  199–200, 265, 267–8
Mary Poppins Comes Back
  (P.L. Travers) 54
Masefield, John: *The Box of*
  Delights 92, 254
Matilda (Roald Dahl) 249–51
meringues 233–4
midnight feasts 144–6
Milly Molly Mandy stories see
  (*The*) *Adventures of Milly-*
  Molly-Mandy (Joyce Lancaster
  Brisley)
Milne, A.A. 265
  Winnie-the-Pooh 126
mollases
  candy pull 139–41
  pies 242–5

Montgomery, L.M.: *Anne of Green*
  Gables 97–8, 120–1, 256
Mr Galliano series (Enid Blyton) 152
muffins 56–9
My Naughty Little Sister (Dorothy
  Edwards) 278–9

N

Naughtiest Girl stories (Enid
  Blyton) 134
Nesbit, E. 88–9
  The Enchanted Castle 188–9
  Five Children and It 260
  The Railway Children 94, 265,
    272–3
Norton, Mary: *The Borrowers* 85

O

onions, fried 78–80
The O'Sullivan Twins (Enid
  Blyton) 144–5, 205

P

pancakes
  Ma's pancake men 22–4
  Swedish 110–11
parkin 270–1
pastry puffs, jam 185–7
patty-pan cake 117–18
Pearce, Philippa: *Tom's Midnight Garden* 76
pickled limes 142–3
picnics 169–70
  picnic pie 242–5
  recipes for 171–95
pies: picnic pie 242–5
pineapple cake 156–8
Pippi Longstocking (Astrid Lindgren) 110, 236, 246–7, 275–6
plums
  ripe 178–9
  stewed 50–1
pocket cache 260–1
Pollyanna (Eleanor H. Porter) 218
porridge, creamy 16–17
Porter, Eleanor H.: *Pollyanna* 218
posset 92–3
potatoes, lid (baked) 81–2

pudding
  rice 90–1
  treacle 99–101

R

The Ragamuffin Mystery (Enid Blyton) 10, 230
The Railway Children (E. Nesbit) 94, 265, 272–3
Ransome, Arthur: Swallows and Amazons stories 149, 154, 159, 162
raspberry cordial 256–7
raspberry jam cakes 199–201
rice pudding 90–1
The Rilloby Fair Mystery (Enid Blyton) 16, 233
ripe plums 178–9
robber tea 254–5
rock buns 239–41
The Rockingdown Mystery (Enid Bltyon) 72, 99
roll (roly-poly), marmalade 60–3
royal icing 272–4
The Rubadub Mystery (Enid Blyton) 74

S

saffron cake 102–4
sandwiches
    cress 176–7
    tomato 180–1
sardines on toast 53
school food 129–30
    recipes for 131–3, 136–46
    tuck box treats 134–5
scones, jam 223–5
The Secret Garden (Frances Hodgson Burnett) 13, 174, 252–3
The Secret of Spiggy Holes (Enid Blyton) 166, 223–4
Secret Seven series (Enid Blyton) 239
seed cake 154–5
Seven Little Australians (Ethel Turner) 182–3
Shackleton, Ernest 162
shortbread 74–5
shrimps, potted 85–7
Slater, Nigel 215
soup, chicken 220
special occasions 265–6
    recipes for 267–83
Spyri, Johanna: *Heidi* 83

squashed fly biscuits 162–4
stewed fruit 49–51
strawberry jam 126–8
Streatfeild, Noel
    Ballet Shoes 123, 258–9
    Dancing Shoes 20, 33
sugar biscuits 230–2
sugar on snow 282–3
sundaes 214–16
supper 77
    a 'funny and delightful' supper 94–5
    recipes for 78–95
Swallows and Amazons stories (Arthur Ransome) 149, 162
    Swallowdale 154, 159
Swedish pancakes 110–11
sweet shops 208–9
The Swish of the Curtain (Pamela Brown) 261
Swiss cheese and bread supper 83–4

T

tarts, jam 30–2
tea time 47–8

ghostbusting tea 76
recipes for 49–75
tipsy trifle 280
toast 52–3
shrimps with 86–7
tomato sandwiches 180–1
Tom's Midnight Garden
(Philippa Pearce) 76
Travers, P.L.
Mary Poppins 199–200, 265, 267–8
Mary Poppins Comes Back 54
treacle pudding 99–101
The Treasure Hunters (Enid
Blyton) 30–1
treats 97–8
going out 197–216
growing up 235–64
kind and thoughtful 217–34
special 99–114, 267–83
trifle 278–81
tuck boxes 134–5
Turkish delight 262–4
Turner, Ethel: Seven Little
Australians 182–3
The Twins at St Clare's series (Enid
Blyton)
The O'Sullivan Twins 144–5, 205

The Twins at St Clare's 144

U

Upper Fourth at Malory Towers (Enid
Blyton) 69

W

walnut cake 41–3
Webster, Jean 130
Daddy Long-Legs 139, 142
What Katy Did (Susan Coolidge)
97, 242–3
What Katy Did at School (Susan
Coolidge) 105–6, 134–5
White, E.B.: Charlotte's Web 18,
285–6
The Wind in the Willows
(Kenneth Grahame) 176
Winnie-the-Pooh (A.A. Milne) 126